FRUITS OF
THE EARTH

THE GREEN HOME

FRUITS OF THE EARTH

100 recipes for jams, jellies, pickles and preserves

GLORIA NICOL
The Laundry

CICO BOOKS

LONDON NEW YORK

For my mum, Alice Nicol, for her
unconditional love, help and support,
without which I would be lost.

Published in 2009 by CICO Books
an imprint of Ryland Peters & Small Ltd
20–21 Jockey's Fields
London WC1R 4BW

www.cicobooks.co.uk

10 9 8 7 6 5 4 3 2 1

A CIP catalogue record for this book is
available from the British Library.

ISBN-13: 978-1-906525-26-2

Printed in China

Project Editor: Gillian Haslam
Text Editors: Alison Bolus and
                    Eleanor Van Zandt
Designer: Barbara Zuñiga
Photographer: Gloria Nicol
Illustrator: Jane Smith
Stylist: Sue Rowlands
(Pages 93, 95, 120 and 125 –
photographer: Winfried Heinze;
stylist: Rose Hammick)

contents

why make jam?

There is something so satisfying about opening a food cupboard, pantry or larder to find the shelves stacked with colourful jars of homemade preserves. These containers of summer and autumn flavours might be just what's required to lift the mood on a dark, gloomy winter's day, when a good dollop of strawberry jam on your bread reminds you of longer, warmer, lighter days. For me, that is what making preserves is all about: capturing the essence of whatever fruit or vegetable it is and sealing that flavour in a jar for another day.

I started making jam 30 or so years ago and have always enjoyed it, despite my fair share of sticky mistakes. It is a traditional part of homemaking that celebrates the seasons and somehow makes life cosier and more comforting. My preserves are handmade and full of chunky pieces, which sets them apart from anything shop-bought. The flavours of the fruits shine through and are rarely masked with spices. Where possible, I reduce the amount of sugar, as the tarter the fruits, the fresher tasting the results.

In the current climate of concerns about being less wasteful, clocking up fewer food miles and eating seasonal, locally grown food, making preserves has never been so popular.

choosing your ingredients

Although strawberries, to give just one example, can now be bought virtually all year round, thanks to the introduction of new varieties, the use of polytunnels and the massive increase in imported produce, nothing beats the flavour of a homegrown strawberry that has ripened in the sun and been picked only moments before. It is this flavour, so sweet and intense, that can be captured in preserves.

Using your own homegrown produce for preserving is hard to beat, as the ingredients will be fresh and you will have control over their growing conditions.

Farmers' markets are another great source. You'll know that the fruit and vegetables have been grown locally and you are more likely to find unusual varieties of produce. Taking advantage of an organic box delivery scheme is another good alternative. Whatever its source, rinse all produce before use.

Food for free

Sometimes ingredients are right in front of your nose, and all you have to do is go out there and find them. Hedgerows and woodlands are full of edible fruits and berries if you know what to look for. You may find crab apples growing wild, along with damsons, greengages or blackberries. Alternatively, if you know someone who grows more fruit than they can use, offer to take it off their hands in exchange for a jar of preserve made using it. It's a win-win situation.

Fruit and pectin

For almost all fruit preserves you need to choose fresh, good-quality, just-ripe fruit in order to achieve the correct pectin content. This is because jam needs the right balance of pectin, acid and sugar to set properly. Different fruits contain varying amounts of pectin, and the pectin content is higher in just-ripe fruit. Fruits high in pectin include crab apples, red, black and white currants, Seville oranges, damsons, gooseberries

and quinces. Fruits low in pectin include strawberries, pears, elderberries, fresh apricots and cherries. Some fruits contain very little pectin, and so jams made using these fruits will need additional help to make them set. Over-ripe fruit can also lower the pectin content, which is why such fruit is not suitable for jams. It is, however, suitable for cordials, so use any fruit that is too ripe for jam to make a delicious cordial or syrup.

The pectin content can be raised in various ways: mixed-fruit jams can use the higher pectin content of one fruit to offset the lower content of another; lemon juice can be added at a rate of the juice of 1–2 lemons to every 2kg (4lb 8oz) fruit, and bottled pectin or special preserving sugar with added pectin can be used.

preserving equipment

The principle underlying all preserving is to prevent decay caused by the growth of yeasts, moulds and bacteria. These organisms are destroyed when heated to sufficiently high temperatures to sterilize them, and, once sterilized, preserves must be kept securely sealed so that air cannot enter. Preserves that contain 60 per cent or more of sugar are less susceptible to the growth of yeasts, which is why jams containing less sugar need eating more quickly.

JAM JARS

Once people discover you are a jam-maker, you will find yourself the happy recipient of empty jam jars of all shapes and sizes. Jars with screw-top lids make the best containers for jams and jellies, while jars with metal clip tops and rubber seals are perfect for potting up chutneys and pickles.

Jars need to be clean and undamaged, without any chips or cracks. Wash them in hot soapy water, then rinse in clean hot water before drying. Place the jars on their sides on a tea towel-covered shelf in the oven and heat to 110°C/225°F/ Gas Mark ¼ for 20–30 minutes, just before using them. They should come out of the oven hot and ready for filling with hot jam.

Always prepare a few more jars than you think you will need, including some tiny jars to hold the last few spoonfuls from the pan.

Corrosive materials must not come into contact with the preserve, especially those containing vinegar, so choose lids that will not corrode if they touch the preserve beneath. This is especially important for chutneys and pickles.

SPECIAL EQUIPMENT

There are a few items you can buy for preserving:

PRESERVING PAN A non-corrosive, non-reactive preserving pan big enough to hold large quantities of boiling jam is a great investment. Often referred to as a maslin pan, a preserving pan should be wide and shallow to encourage rapid evaporation when bringing jam to setting point. A good-quality pan will have a thick, heavy base that will prevent any preserve from burning. While copper and aluminium pans are both popular, I think stainless steel is best, and it is certainly necessary when making preserves that contain vinegar.

When jam is brought to a rolling boil it rises up in the pan, so never over-fill the pan. If the pan is too small and overfilled, you will either end up with an overflowing mess of boiling syrupy jam or, in order to prevent this happening, you won't be able to raise the temperature high enough to reach setting point.

DOUBLE BOILER Useful when making fruit curds and fruit syrups and cordials, though can be replaced by a bowl set over a pan of simmering water.

Pickles and chutneys both require vinegars flavoured with spices, and all the recipes in this book give instructions for making these from scratch. However, you can also make your own vinegars using the recipes on the right – two for pickling vinegars and two for sweetened pickling vinegars, which are suitable for pickling fruits and fruit chutneys.

PICKLING VINEGAR

To 1 litre (1¾ pints) cider, malt or wine vinegar, add:
20g (¾oz) fresh root ginger, peeled and finely sliced
1 tbsp each black peppercorns, mustard seeds,
   celery seeds
8 dried red chillies
2 tsp each whole allspice, whole cloves, whole
   coriander seeds

Mix all the spices together and divide between clean, sterilized bottles. Top up the bottles with the vinegar and seal with corks or stoppers. Leave the vinegar to infuse for 6–8 weeks, giving the bottles the occasional shake. Strain the spices from the vinegar before using.

For a quicker version:

Place all the ingredients in a bowl and place over a pan of simmering water, or use a double boiler. Allow the vinegar to warm through without boiling, then remove it from the heat and leave the spices to steep in the warm vinegar for 2–3 hours. Strain the spices from the vinegar before using.

SWEET PICKLING VINEGAR

To 1 litre (1¾ pints) cider, malt or wine vinegar, add:
1 cinnamon stick
1 tbsp each whole allspice, whole coriander seeds,
   whole cloves, white peppercorns
5 blades of mace
2 dried red chillies (optional)
800g (1lb 12oz) brown or white sugar

Mix the spices together and divide between clean bottles. Warm the vinegar and dissolve the sugar in it, then top up the bottles with the vinegar and seal with corks or stoppers. Leave to infuse for 6–8 weeks, giving the bottles the occasional shake. Strain the spices from the vinegar before using.

For a quicker version:

Place 600ml (1 pint) white wine vinegar, 200g (7oz) sugar, 1cm (⅜in) square piece of fresh root ginger, a few whole allspice berries and black peppercorns in a pan and stir over a low heat to dissolve the sugar. Turn up the heat and boil for 1 minute, then remove from the heat. Strain the spices from the vinegar before using.

MAKING CORDIALS AND SYRUPS

Cordials and syrups make good use of fruit that is over-ripe and not suitable for jam-making; they are also easy to make. Soft fruits such as blackberries, blackcurrants, loganberries and raspberries are suitable, as are citrus fruits and foraged fruits such as rosehips, elderflowers and elderberries.

For all soft fruits the method is the same. Put the fruit in a bowl and break it up with a spoon, then add only the minimal amount of water, if any at all. Place the bowl over a pan of simmering water and heat through to extract all the juice from the fruit. Pour the fruit through a jelly bag and collect the juice underneath, leaving it to drip overnight.

Add 350g (12oz) sugar to every 500ml (17fl oz) juice and stir together over a low heat until dissolved; do not allow it to boil. Strain into clean bottles, filling to within 2.5cm (1in) of the top of the bottle. Cork securely or use bottles with ceramic stoppers and wires. The bottles will now need to be sterilized so that they keep for a long time. (Alternatively, and this is the easier option, the syrup or cordial can be poured into suitable containers and frozen.)

To sterilize, place some folded newspaper or a trivet in the bottom of a pan and place the bottles on top. Add cold water almost to the top of the bottles, then bring to the boil and simmer for 20 minutes. Make sure that the bottles are securely sealed, then store them in a cool, dry place.

KEEPING TIMES

The jams and jellies will keep, unopened, in a cool, dark place for at least 6 months, and the other preserves will keep for 6–12 months. Keeping times will vary once jars and bottles are opened, but you'll find that these preserves are so delicious that they will be eaten up long before there is any chance of them deteriorating.

PROBLEM SOLVING

Why jam goes mouldy

Mould is most often caused by a failure to cover the jam with a waxed disc while it is still very hot. Alternatively, jars may have been damp or cold when used, weren't filled right to the top or have been stored in a damp place. Other possible causes are insufficient evaporation of water during the preliminary cooking and/or too short a period of boiling after the sugar has been added. Jam with a good set is less likely to go mouldy, while a softer-set jam will be more inclined to spoil. Sometimes mould can form because the fruit was picked on a wet day. Mould is not harmful to the jam but it may affect the taste slightly. If it is removed, the jam can be boiled up again and re-potted in clean, sterilized jars.

Why tiny bubbles appear

Bubbles indicate fermentation, which is usually the result of too little sugar in relation to the quantity of fruit. When jam is not reduced sufficiently, this can also affect the proportion of sugar.

Why fruit rises in the jam

When the fruit is in big pieces or used whole, such as strawberries, the pieces tend to rise in the jam after potting. To keep them dispersed throughout the preserve, leave the jam in the pan for 10–15 minutes after setting point is reached to thicken slightly, then stir before pouring it into the pots. The syrupy consistency of softer-set jams means that fruit will invariably rise. The same problem may occur with rind in marmalade – the solution of waiting and stirring is the same.

Why jam crystallizes

Too much sugar or too little acid are usually the cause. Low-acid fruits benefit from the addition of acid in the form of lemon juice. Making sure that the sugar has dissolved completely before bringing the jam to a fast boil also helps. Sometimes over-ripe fruit is responsible or storing the jam in too warm a place.

Why jam won't set

Low levels of pectin due to using fruits containing very little pectin or over-ripe fruit make it difficult to reach setting point. Other reasons include under-boiling the fruit, so the pectin is not fully extracted, or insufficient evaporation of the water before the sugar is added, in which case return the jam to the preserving pan and boil it further. It is also possible to over-cook jam after sugar has been added, for which there is no remedy. For fruits low in pectin, such as strawberries and cherries, you can add more pectin in the form of fruits (such as lemon juice, apples or redcurrants), bottled pectin or preserving sugar, which has added pectin.

Why jam shrinks in the jar

Shrinkage is caused by the jam being inadequately covered or sealed or failure to store it in a cool, dark and dry place.

jams

We need jam to spread on our bread, make a filling for a sponge cake and to ooze over a steamed pudding. Jam is simply a term used to describe fruit and sugar cooked together so it will keep, and can include the fruit in pieces or be made from puréed fruit. It is a little added extra in life that happens to make life that bit sweeter.

Makes 1.2kg (2lb 12oz)
1kg (2lb 4oz) blackberries
1 star anise
3 cloves
1 small cinnamon stick
juice of 2 lemons
700g (1lb 9oz) warmed sugar (see page 10)

spiced blackberry jam

I don't often choose to spice up the fruits when jam making, preferring the simple fruit flavours to dominate. However, here a handful of warming spices suits this autumnal foraged fruit preserve down to the ground.

1 Place the blackberries in a saucepan with the star anise, cloves, cinnamon stick and 2 tablespoons water (just enough so the fruit doesn't catch on the pan). Bring them to simmering point and continue cooking until they are tender and juicy, mashing them with a spoon.

2 Remove the cinnamon stick and press the berries through the fine disc of a food mill or a sieve. If you prefer a chunkier-textured jam, there is no need to purée the fruit at all: simply fish out the spices with a spoon and continue with the whole blackberry pulp.

3 Add the lemon juice to the blackberries and place them in a preserving pan; heat through, stirring gently. Add the warmed sugar to the pan and stir until completely dissolved, then turn up the heat and boil the jam rapidly to reach setting point (see page 10). Skim if necessary (see page 11).

4 Pour the jam into hot, sterilized jars (see page 8) and seal (see page 11).

Makes 1.5kg (3lb 5oz)
900g (2lb) blackberries
1 star anise
3 cloves
1 small cinnamon stick

4 nectarines (approx. 430g/15oz when
 skinned and stoned)
juice of 2 lemons
900g (2lb) warmed sugar (see page 10)

spiced blackberry & nectarine jam

I discovered this combination when I found a bargain pack of nectarines at the supermarket. They bring a welcome sharpness to the mellow flavour of blackberries as well as an appealing texture.

Cook and purée the blackberries and spices as in steps 1–2 on page 16. To skin the nectarines, place them in a bowl and pour boiling water over them. Leave for a few minutes, then drain off the water and replace with cold water; the skins should slip easily off the fruit. Cut the nectarines into quarters, removing the stones, then cut each quarter into thirds (smaller pieces if you like a finer-textured preserve). Place the blackberries, lemon juice, nectarines and sugar in a preserving pan and cook as in step 3 on page 16. Leave the jam for 5 minutes, then stir to redistribute the nectarine pieces. Pot and seal the jam as before.

Makes 1.3kg (3lb)
1kg (2lb 4oz) apricots
800g (1lb 12oz) sugar
juice of 1 lemon

apricot jam

This apricot jam contains slightly less sugar than most, resulting in a softer set, and the apricots are left in big chunks. Because of this, it is inevitable that the fruit will rise to the top of the jar, rather than being suspended evenly throughout the jam. No matter: you can simply allocate an apricot half for every serving. One apricot piece will squash perfectly under the knife to fill a scone, for example. The cooking time is kept to a minimum, so keeping the flavour at its utmost.

1 Skin the fruits by placing them in a bowl, pouring boiling water over them and leaving them for a few minutes, then replacing the hot water with cold. The skins should then be easy to peel away. Keep the skins to one side. Halve the fruits and remove the stones. Place the skins and stones in a piece of muslin and tie it into a bag with string.

2 Place the sugar and lemon juice in a ceramic or glass bowl and add 200ml (7fl oz) water; tuck the muslin bag in among the other ingredients. Push a piece of greaseproof paper down onto the surface to cover it and leave the bowl in the fridge overnight.

3 By the next day the juice will have been drawn out of the fruits into the sugar, which will be partly dissolved. Pour the contents of the bowl into a preserving pan and heat gently, stirring all the time until the sugar has completely dissolved. Simmer gently for 10 minutes without stirring so the apricot halves stay intact, then remove them from the syrup using a slotted spoon. Remove and discard the muslin bag.

4 Bring the syrup to the boil and boil rapidly to reach setting point (see page 10), then quickly put the apricots back into the syrup and bring to the boil again. Remove the jam from the heat. Skim if necessary (see page 11).

5 Spoon the apricots into hot, sterilized jars (see page 8), dividing them equally, then pour the syrup over them, filling the jars up to the top. Seal the jars (see page 11) and leave them to cool upside down.

Makes 1.3kg (3lb)
1 vanilla pod
1kg (2lb 4oz) apricots

800g (1lb 12oz) sugar
juice of 1 lemon

apricot & vanilla jam

This combination seems so French to me. With its softer syrupy set, you may be tempted to eat this delicious preserve as a dessert without the need for any bread – just add a dollop of crème fraîche.

First slice the vanilla pod in half lengthways and scrape out the seeds with the blade of a knife. Then follow the instructions for Apricot Jam, adding the seeds to the ingredients when placing them in a bowl and tucking the pod pieces in among the fruit before leaving the mixture to macerate overnight. Remove the pod pieces before filling and sealing the jars.

Makes 1.3kg (3lb)
1kg (2lb 4oz) white currants
4 red gooseberries (optional)
juice of 1 lemon
2 red chillies (or more if you wish),
　　deseeded and finely chopped
warmed sugar (see page 10; for quantity
　　see step 3)

white currant & red chilli jam

White currants are another fruit with a lovely tart flavour, which makes them just perfect for jam making. This jam, with its additional chilli kick, is subtle enough to eat on sourdough toast for breakfast but could also be taken up a notch, by adding more chilli to taste, and serving as a relish to go with cheese. And if you have a few red gooseberries to add to the currants, they'll give this jam a beautiful rose hue.

1 Strip the white currants from their stalks by running the tines of a fork through their stems. Place the currants and gooseberries, if using, in a pan along with the lemon juice and 150ml (5fl oz) water. Simmer until the fruits are soft and bursting.

2 Push the fruit through the fine disc of a food mill or a sieve, collecting the resulting purée in a measuring jug.

3 Allow 450g (1lb) sugar to every 600ml (1 pint) of purée.

4 Gently heat the purée and add the chopped chillies, then the warmed sugar. Stir the jam over a low heat until the sugar has completely dissolved. Turn up the heat and boil rapidly to reach setting point (see page 10). Skim if necessary (see page 11).

5 Pour the jam into hot, sterilized jars (see page 8) and seal (see page 11).

22 **jams**

Makes 1.3kg (3lb)
1kg (2lb 4oz) raspberries
juice of 1 lemon
800g (1lb 12oz) warmed sugar (see page 10)

raspberry jam

Some people like jam with lots of seeds in it; some don't. With raspberry jam you have a choice. If you love the flavour of this fruit but find the seeds annoying, push the softened fruit through a sieve for a smoother finish. The result will taste just as good as the kind with the seeds in it.

1 Place the raspberries and lemon juice in a preserving pan. Heat them gently to draw out the juice, mashing the berries with a spoon until the fruit is soft and there is plenty of juice. If you want a smooth jam, push the fruit through a sieve to remove the seeds.

2 Add the warmed sugar to the fruit and stir over a gentle heat until the sugar has completely dissolved. Turn up the heat and bring the jam to a fast boil until it reaches setting point (see page 10). Skim if necessary (see page 11).

3 Pour the jam into hot, sterilized jars (see page 8) and seal (see page 11).

Makes 1.5kg (3lb 5oz)
450g (1lb) gooseberries
450g (1lb) strawberries, hulled
900g (2lb) warmed sugar (see page 10)
juice of 1 lemon

strawberry & gooseberry jam

Gooseberries and strawberries make a good partnership as the higher pectin levels found in gooseberries offset the lower levels in the strawberries. My personal preference is also for a jam which not only tastes great but that is colourful as well, and this unusual combination certainly ticks all those boxes.

1 Place the gooseberries in a preserving pan with 3 tablespoons of water. Heat gently and simmer until the berries are just soft, then add the strawberries. Cook for 5 minutes until the fruits begin to lose their shape and the juice starts to run.

2 Add the warmed sugar and the lemon juice to the fruit. Stir gently over a low heat until the sugar has completely dissolved. Turn up the heat and boil rapidly to reach setting point (see page 10). Skim if necessary (see page 11).

3 Pour the jam into hot, sterilized jars (see page 8) and seal (see page 11).

Makes 1.3kg (3lb)
1 vanilla pod
1kg (2lb 4oz) strawberries, hulled; larger
    fruits halved
750g (1lb 10oz) sugar
juice of 3 lemons

strawberry & vanilla jam

Let's face it, strawberry jam is the real classic. This fragile fruit isn't a great keeper, so for the best jam, capture the fruit at its freshest, preserving it in recognizable chunks. This really is summer in a jar. Here I have teamed strawberries with vanilla, the perfect partner, which as far as I'm concerned you can't ever get enough of.

This recipe uses slightly less sugar than a traditional strawberry jam might and consequently has a softer set, which means if you are feeling really gluttonous, you can eat it straight from the jar. Or swirl a few spoonfuls through a mixture of mascarpone and plain yoghurt for a fast pudding. Or dollop it onto a freshly baked scone – eating it quickly before the jam oozes away over the sides.

1 Split the vanilla pod lengthways into four pieces and place in a bowl with the strawberries, tucking the pod pieces in among the fruit. Cover with the sugar and leave for 12 hours or overnight.

2 Pour the fruit, vanilla pod and juice into a preserving pan and add the lemon juice. Cook over a low heat until the sugar has dissolved, stirring only now and then so that the fruit stays intact. Turn up the heat and boil rapidly to reach setting point (see page 10). Skim if necessary (see page 11).

3 Remove the vanilla pod pieces, scrape the seeds out of them and add these to the jam, disposing of the pods. Stir the seeds through the jam.

4 Pour the jam into hot, sterilized jars (see page 8) and seal (see page 11).

Makes 750g (1lb 10oz)
450g (1lb) plums, halved and stoned
450g (1lb) warmed sugar (see page 10)

plum jam

Where I live we have our own, locally grown plum variety, the Blaisdon Red plum, so naturally that is my own particular favourite for this jam. Most years, come late summer, the trees are dripping with them, so there is always lots of jam making to be done. Of course, other plum varieties will do just as well.

1 Place the plums in a pan with 100ml (3½fl oz) water and bring to a simmer, then cook gently for 10 minutes until the plums are soft but still intact.

2 Add the warmed sugar to the fruit and stir over a low heat until all the sugar has dissolved, then turn up the heat and boil rapidly to reach setting point (see page 10). Skim if necessary (see page 11).

3 Pour the jam into hot, sterilized jars (see page 8) and seal (see page 11).

damson jam

Damsons make superb jam, one of the best. It is an old fashioned fruit, which isn't so often used commercially for preserving. The bold and traditional character of this fruit makes it ideal as a single fruit jam.

Follow the recipe for Plum Jam using damsons, but do not attempt to remove the stones before cooking. Spoon off any stones that float to the surface, then leave the cooked fruit to cool before using your hands to find and remove the rest. Once you are sure you have removed all the stones, add the sugar and bring to setting point as before.

Makes 1.5kg (3lb 5oz)
450g (1lb) plums, halved and stoned

450g (1lb) marrow flesh, cut
  into chunks
900g (2lb) sugar

plum & marrow jam

A great jam to help make just a few plums go a long way. Marrow acts as a chameleon here, bulking out the jam and soaking up the fruity sweetness of the plums.

Put the plums and marrow together in a pan with 100ml (3½fl oz) water and continue as for Plum Jam.

Makes 1.65kg (3lb 10oz)
700g (1lb 9oz) raspberries
700g (1lb 9oz) ripe peaches (about 6)
1kg (2lb 4oz) sugar
juice of 2 large lemons

peach & raspberry jam

This jam is not only wonderfully fragrant but also gloriously colourful, with a combination of deep red raspberries dotted through with peach pieces. Here, as usual, I would opt for a chunky texture to set this preserve apart from anything you will ever find in a shop. You can, of course, chop the peaches finer if you prefer.

1 Place the raspberries in a pan. Warm them gently to soften them and release their juice, mashing them with the back of a spoon.

2 When they are soft and juicy, push them through the fine disc of a food mill or a sieve.

3 Place the raspberry purée, 500g (1 1lb 2oz) of the sugar and half of the lemon juice in a pan and bring to a simmer, then remove from the heat and pour into a ceramic or glass bowl. Cover the surface with greaseproof paper, pushed down onto the fruit, and leave the bowl in the fridge overnight.

4 Meanwhile, to skin the peaches, place them in a bowl and pour boiling water over them. Leave to steep for a few minutes, then pour off the water and replace with cold water; the skins should now easily peel away from the flesh. Cut the peaches into quarters and remove the stones, then cut each quarter in half, so the pieces are still quite chunky.

5 Place the peaches, remaining sugar and lemon juice in a pan, bring just to simmering point, then remove from the heat. Pour the fruit into a glass or ceramic bowl and cover it with greaseproof paper as described for the raspberries; leave in the fridge overnight.

6 The next day, combine the raspberries and peaches in a preserving pan and heat gently, stirring all the time to be sure that the sugar has completely dissolved. Turn up the heat and boil rapidly until setting point is reached (see page 10). Skim if necessary (see page 11). Leave for 5 minutes, then stir to distribute the peach pieces. Pour the jam into hot, sterilized jars (see page 8) and seal (see page 11).

Makes 900g (2lb)
700g (1lb 9oz) cherries
500g (1lb 2oz) warmed sugar (see page 10)
1 tbsp lemon juice

cherry jam

You can use a black cooking cherry, such as a Morello cherry for this jam, or a paler dessert cherry and the colour of your jam will vary accordingly. If you grow your own, make sure to pick them as soon as they ripen or else the birds will eat the lot before you get the chance.

1 Pit the cherries using a cherry stoner over a basin to catch any juice. Place the stones in a piece of muslin and tie it into a bag with string. Put the fruit and juice into a pan with 2 tablespoons water and simmer gently until the fruit is just cooked.

2 Add the warmed sugar and the lemon juice to the fruit and stir over a low heat until all the sugar has dissolved, then turn up the heat and boil rapidly to reach setting point (see page 10). Remove the muslin bag and leave the jam for 5–10 minutes, then stir to redistribute the cherries. Skim if necessary (see page 11).

3 Pour the jam into hot, sterilized jars (see page 8) and seal (see page 11).

Makes 2.5kg (5lb 8oz)
250g (9oz) rosehips
250g (9oz) hawthorn hips ('haws')
250g (9oz) rowan berries
250g (9oz) sloes

450g (1lb) crab apples or tart cooking
   apples, chopped
450g (1lb) blackberries
450g (1lb) elderberries
125g (4oz) hazelnuts, shelled and chopped
warmed sugar (see page 10; for quantity
   see step 3)

hedgerow jam

Foraging is such a satisfying pursuit – gathering food for free that has required no effort whatsoever to cultivate. Whether there is any produce to be had is entirely in nature's hands, and the autumnal fruits may well be either bountiful or scarce, varying from year to year. Hedgerow jam makes use of lots of ingredients, but the medley can be changed based on what is readily available. As not all of the fruits for this recipe may be ripe at just the same time, you will need a flexible approach. Sloes are generally best picked after a first frost, by which time elderberries will have been and gone. Of course, not all berries are edible, so if you don't know how to recognize the ones that are, then this jam isn't for you. Hedgerow Jam is autumn in a jar.

1 Pick over the fruit and remove the stalks. Place the hips, haws, rowan berries, sloes and apples in a pan with just enough water to cover the fruit, so it just begins to float. Simmer for approximately 15 minutes until the fruit is soft and the apples fluffy.

2 Push the fruit mixture through the fine disc of a food mill or a sieve and collect the puréed pulp in a preserving pan. Add the blackberries, elderberries and nuts and simmer for 15 minutes.

3 Measure the cooked fruit and add an equal amount of warmed sugar. Stir over a low heat until all the sugar has dissolved, then turn up the heat and boil rapidly to reach setting point (see page 10). Skim if necessary (see page 11).

4 Pour the jam into hot, sterilized jars (see page 8) and seal (see page 11).

Makes 1.3kg (3lb)
1kg (2lb 4oz) pears, peeled, cored and cut
  into chunky slices
juice of 2 lemons
750g (1lb 10oz) sugar
1 vanilla pod

pear & vanilla jam

This jam is another of my particular favourites and is one I find it hard to live without. The specks of real vanilla dotted throughout the pale jam show its quality, infusing their aromatic flavour. Here, macerating the pears also brings out the most flavour from the fruit.

1 Place the pears in a bowl with the lemon juice to stop them discolouring. Sprinkle the sugar over the fruit and add 200ml (7fl oz) water.

2 Slice the vanilla pod in half lengthways and scrape out the seeds, then tuck the pod in among the pears and add the seeds. Cover the bowl with a plate and leave overnight for the sugar to soak up some of the juices from the fruit.

3 The next day, pour the contents of the bowl into a preserving pan and stir over a low heat until the sugar has dissolved, then turn up the heat and boil rapidly to reach setting point (see page 10), by which time the pear pieces will be translucent. Skim if necessary (see page 11).

4 Remove the vanilla pod, then pour the jam into hot, sterilized jars (see page 8) and seal (see page 11).

pear & chocolate jam

After holidaying in France, my neighbours brought back some pear jam which had tiny nuggets of chocolate suspended through the syrup. This is my interpretation of that unusual preserve.

Coarsely grate 150g (5oz) good-quality dark chocolate. Make the Pear & Vanilla Jam and spoon it into the jars in layers interspersed with sprinkled grated chocolate. The chocolate will melt on contact with the hot jam, but the aim is to have chocolate speckled throughout, rather then mixed in, so that the overall colour of the jam is pale.

Makes 1.65kg (3lb 10oz)
1kg (2lb 4oz) pumpkin or butternut
    squash flesh
1 vanilla pod
1kg (2lb 4oz) sugar
juice of 2 lemons

pumpkin & vanilla jam

This recipe is a great one to make when you are faced with a pile of scooped-out pumpkin innards after making Halloween lanterns. The natural sweetness of the pumpkin flesh is just perfect for making into jam.

1 Place the pumpkin in a pan with just enough water to stop it catching and cook over a moderate heat for 10–15 minutes until it is cooked through but still retains its shape. Drain off any excess juices and, when the pumpkin is cool enough to handle, chop it into finer pieces.

2 Slice the vanilla pod in half lengthways and scrape out the seeds with the blade of a knife. Place the pumpkin, sugar and lemon juice in a bowl, tuck the vanilla pod pieces in among the pumpkin and add the seeds. Cover with a piece of greaseproof paper pushed down onto the surface and leave overnight.

3 The next day, pour the contents of the bowl into a preserving pan and stir over a low heat until all the sugar has dissolved, then turn up the heat and boil rapidly to reach setting point (see page 10). Skim if necessary (see page 11).

4 Pour the jam into hot, sterilized jars (see page 8) and seal (see page 11).

Makes 1.3kg (3lb)
500g (1lb 2oz) apricots
500g (1lb 2oz) rhubarb, cut into short lengths
750g (1lb 10oz) sugar
juice of 1 lemon

rhubarb & apricot jam

This jam is an absolute star. Everyone who has tasted it has been knocked out by how full of flavour it is and the perfection of this combination of fruits. The pinkness of the rhubarb pieces along with the chunky apricot halves also makes it a real treat visually. If you make only one jam in this book (hopefully you'll make more than that!), this is the one.

1 Skin the apricots by placing them in a bowl and pouring boiling water over them. Leave for a few minutes, then drain the water and replace with cold water. The skins should then be easy to peel away with a knife. Cut into halves and remove the stones.

2 Place all the ingredients in a bowl, cover with a plate and leave for 1 hour.

3 Pour the contents of the bowl into a preserving pan and stir over a low heat to dissolve the sugar. Turn up the heat and bring just to simmering point, then remove from the heat. Pour everything into a glass or ceramic bowl, cover with a piece of greaseproof paper pushed down onto the surface and leave overnight in the fridge.

4 The next day, pour the contents of the bowl back into the preserving pan and stir over a low heat until all the sugar has dissolved, then turn up the heat and boil rapidly to reach setting point (see page 10). Skim if necessary (see page 11).

5 Pour the jam into hot, sterilized jars (see page 8) and seal (see page 11).

Makes 1.4kg (3lb 2oz)
1kg (2lb 4oz) rhubarb, cut into short lengths

finely grated zest and juice of 3 limes
850g (1lb 14oz) sugar

rhubarb & lime jam

Rhubarb is often teamed up with orange, but I much prefer to combine it with lime instead. This is a medley made in heaven.

Place all the ingredients in a bowl, cover with a plate and leave for 1 hour. Then follow steps 3–5 of Rhubarb & Apricot Jam.

Makes 750g (1lb 10oz)
450g (1lb) figs, stalks removed and
 chopped into small pieces

450g (1lb) warmed sugar (see page 10)
 juice of 1 lemon

green fig jam

Green or purple figs are suitable for jam making. Figs do not ripen any further once picked from
the tree, and they don't have a massive flavour when unripe, so pick or buy them already ripe
enough to use. This jam has a beautiful rich colour and is dotted throughout with seeds.

1 Place the figs in a pan with 2 tablespoons water, heat gently to a simmer and
cook until soft and juicy.

2 Add the warmed sugar and the lemon juice to the fruit and stir over a low heat
until all the sugar has dissolved, then turn up the heat and boil rapidly to reach
setting point (see page 10). Leave for 10 minutes, then stir to distribute the fig
pieces throughout the jam. Skim if necessary (see page 11).

3 Pour the jam into hot, sterilized jars (see page 8) and seal (see page 11).

Makes 1.4kg (3lb 2oz)
600g (1lb 5oz) figs
400g (14oz) pears, peeled, cored and diced
finely grated zest and juice of 1 large orange
 and 1 lemon

850g (1lb 14oz) sugar
8 green cardamom pods, crushed
 and pods discarded

fig & pear jam

Both main ingredients here are low in pectin so definitely need help from the lemon and orange
additions to boost their setting power. Green cardamom seeds add a unique and unusual twist.

Prepare the figs as above, then place all ingredients in a bowl and leave for 1 hour.
Pour into a preserving pan, stir over a low heat to dissolve the sugar. then turn up
the heat and bring to simmering point. Pour into a glass or ceramic bowl, cover
with greaseproof paper pushed down onto the surface and leave overnight in the
fridge. Next day, pour the contents back into the pan and stir over a low heat, then
turn up the heat and boil rapidly to reach setting point (see page 10). Pot as above.

Makes 700g (1lb 9oz)
juice and finely pared rind of 1 lemon
500g (1lb 2oz) green tomatoes, finely
chopped
400g (14oz) sugar
2 pieces of stem ginger, finely sliced

green tomato jam

Usually thought of as an ingredient for chutney, green tomatoes were once popular for jam making but have somehow fallen from favour. This recipe will prove that a fashion revival is due. The lemon peel and stem ginger work well here to produce a candied jam with a fabulous colour.

1 Place the rind in a pan with just enough water to cover it and simmer for about 1 hour until soft. Drain the rind, discarding the liquid.

2 Place the tomatoes and lemon juice in a bowl with the sugar and leave overnight for the sugar to soak up some of the juices from the fruit.

3 Next day, pour the contents of the bowl into a preserving pan and add the rind. Stir over a low heat until the sugar has dissolved, then turn up the heat and boil rapidly to reach setting point (see page 10). Skim if necessary (see page 11).

4 Stir in the stem ginger, then pour the jam into hot, sterilized jars (see page 8) and seal (see page 11).

green tomato & angelica jam

I came across this combination in *Tomatoes and How to Grow Them* by F R Castle, dated 1938. Angelica is an interesting herb to grow and makes a towering plant showy enough to work in the herbaceous border. If you don't have fresh angelica, you may be able to buy candied stems.

Use 50g (2oz) fresh stems or 30g (1¼oz) candied pieces and follow the recipe for Green Tomato Jam, omitting the stem ginger. If using fresh angelica, choose young stems, pour boiling water over them and allow to steep for 5 minutes before draining and shredding finely. Add to the tomatoes at the beginning. For candied stems, chop finely and add at the end of the recipe instead of the stem ginger.

Makes 1.65kg (3lb 10oz)
250g (9oz) blackcurrants
250g (9oz) redcurrants
250g (9oz) strawberries
250g (9oz) raspberries
1kg (2lb 4oz) warmed sugar (see page 10)

tutti frutti jam

Mixed-fruit jams are a good way of using up small amounts of fruits that aren't in a great enough quantity to make jam on their own. You can also combine fruits with lower pectin levels with others that have a higher pectin content, which is an ideal way of helping the jam to set.

1 Strip the black and redcurrants from their stalks by running the tines of a fork through the stems. Place the currants in a preserving pan with enough water just to stop the fruits catching on the bottom of the pan. Bring to the boil, then simmer for 15–20 minutes.

2 Add the strawberries and raspberries and simmer for a further 10 minutes. Add the warmed sugar to the fruit and stir over a low heat until all the sugar has dissolved. Turn up the heat and boil rapidly to reach setting point (see page 10). Skim if necessary (see page 11).

3 Pour the jam into hot, sterilized jars (see page 8) and seal (see page 11).

Makes 1.3kg (3lb)
1kg (2lb 4oz) gooseberries, topped
  and tailed

800g (1lb 12oz) sugar
juice of 2 lemons

gooseberry jam

Gooseberries make a sharp jam that works equally well as a sweet or savoury accompaniment. The first varieties, ready to pick in early summer, herald the beginning of a season of luscious fruits and their tartness makes them ideal for jam making. Later varieties get sweeter and can be eaten raw.

1 Place all the ingredients in a preserving pan and heat gently until simmering. Remove immediately from the heat and pour the contents into a ceramic or glass bowl. Cover the surface with greaseproof paper, pushing it down onto the fruit. Leave the bowl overnight in the refrigerator.

2 The next day, pour the contents of the bowl back into the preserving pan and heat gently, stirring to be sure that all the sugar has dissolved. Then turn up the heat and boil rapidly to reach setting point (see page 10). This takes very little time to achieve – only 5–10 minutes – and you need to watch that the syrup doesn't burn. Skim if necessary (see page 11).

3 Pour the jam into hot, sterilized jars (see page 8) and seal (see page 11).

Makes 1.3kg (3lb)
good handful of fresh elderflowers
1kg (2lb 4oz) gooseberries, topped
  and tailed

800g (1lb 12oz) sugar
juice of 2 lemons

gooseberry & elderflower jam

How convenient that elderflowers are in season at the same time as early gooseberries. Here, again, elderflowers bring their unique and delicate flavour to a classic pairing.

First, shake the flowers, face down, to remove any unwanted creatures, then wrap them in a piece of muslin and tie into a bundle. Follow the recipe for Gooseberry Jam, pushing the elderflower bundle in among the gooseberries during their initial simmer and when being left to macerate overnight. Remove the bundle before the fruit is returned to the preserving pan for the final cooking time.

Makes 1.35kg (3lb 1oz)
500g (1lb 2oz) peaches, quartered
    and stoned
500g (1lb 2oz) pears, quartered
juice of 1 lemon
850g (1lb 14oz) sugar

peach & pear jam

This is another beautiful combination of delicate flavours. Here I have used a food mill to process the fruits, as I like the texture this method gives to the jam and it cuts down on the initial preparation. You can, however, leave the fruits in whole chunks if you prefer, in which case you will need to peel and core the pears and skin and stone the peaches first.

1 Place the fruit in a pan with the lemon juice plus 1 tablespoon water and heat gently to release the juices and soften the fruit. Simmer for 10 minutes, then remove from the heat and leave to cool.

2 Press the fruit mixture through the fine disc of a food mill or a sieve and collect the puréed pulp in a preserving pan. Add the sugar to the fruit and stir over a low heat until all the sugar has dissolved, then turn up the heat and boil rapidly to reach setting point (see page 10). Skim if necessary (see page 11).

3 Pour the jam into hot, sterilized jars (see page 8) and seal (see page 11).

Makes 2.1kg (4lb 12oz)
500g (1lb 2oz) cooking apples,
  roughly chopped
500g (1lb 2oz) pears, roughly chopped
500g (1lb 2oz) plums, halved
300ml (10½fl oz) water
zest and juice of 1 lemon
25g (1oz) root ginger, bruised
2 cloves
1.25kg (2lb 12oz) sugar

dumpsideary jam

Dumpsideary jam comes with an endearing name that smacks of tradition and uses a sumptuous medley of orchard fruits – apples, pears and plums – that are in season together. Lightly spiced with ginger and cloves, it is sometimes known as High Dumpsideary while a similar jam without the spices is called mixty maxty. When you give a jar of this jam to someone, the name alone is sure to be a talking point.

1 Place all the fruits and the plum stones in a preserving pan along with 300ml (10½fl oz) water and simmer gently until soft.

2 Remove the plum stones, then press all the fruit through the fine disc of a food mill or a sieve.

3 Place the resulting fruit purée in a preserving pan and add the lemon zest and juice. Tie the spices in a piece of muslin and add this to the pan along with the sugar. Heat the mixture slowly, stirring until the sugar has completely dissolved. Turn up the heat and boil rapidly to reach setting point (see page 10). Skim if necessary (see page 11).

4 Remove the spices. Pour the jam pour into hot, sterilized jars (see page 8) and seal (see page 11).

jellies

Made from the juices extracted from the fruit, jellies have a clarity and purity that is very attractive. From the amber hues of crab apple, the glorious ruby shades of raspberry and redcurrant and the dense blackness of blackcurrant and blackberry jellies, when you hold the jar up to the light it is like gazing through stained glass.

For quantity, see page 12

1kg (2lb 4oz) blackcurrants
juice of 1 lemon (optional)
warmed sugar (see page 10; for quantity
   see step 5)

blackcurrant jelly

This jelly is deep black and glassy, with a perfectly balanced rich, yet tart, flavour. Blackcurrants have an unmistakable and robust taste that makes them ideal for jams and jellies. (If you prefer a slightly less tart version you can omit the lemon juice.) This one is especially suitable for anyone who prefers a smooth, 'no bits' spread; it is great on toast for breakfast and also makes an excellent filling for a sandwich cake.

1 Strip the blackcurrants from their stalks by running the tines of a fork through their stems.

2 Place the currants in a preserving pan with the lemon juice, if using, and 600ml (1 pint) water and simmer for 5 minutes until the currants start to burst and the juice flows. Remove from the heat and squash the currants with a fork.

3 Pour the currants and liquid into a jelly bag suspended over a bowl and leave it to drip for several hours or overnight (resisting the urge to help things along by squeezing the bag).

4 As blackcurrants have a high pectin content (see page 7), you can then increase the yield by tipping the pulp back into the preserving pan, along with 300ml (10fl oz) water, and boiling it for 5 minutes. Pour the pulp back into the jelly bag and leave it to drain for a few hours to extract the juice, collecting it in a measuring jug.

5 Allow 450g (1lb) sugar for every 600ml (1 pint) juice.

6 Heat the juice in a preserving pan over a low heat, then add the warmed sugar. Stir until the sugar has completely dissolved, then turn up the heat and boil rapidly until setting point is reached (see page 10). Skim if necessary (see page 11). Pour into hot, sterilized jars (see page 8) and seal (see page 11).

redcurrant & gooseberry jelly

Gooseberries are almost top of the list for pectin content with redcurrants not too far behind, so you can expect your jelly to have a good set. The redcurrants help to give this jelly a good colour, which the gooseberries alone don't have.

Follow the recipe for Blackcurrant Jelly, but use 500g (1lb 2oz) each of redcurrants and gooseberries and 400ml (14fl oz) water. Boil the currants and berries together until soft and bursting, then pour into a jelly bag and collect the juice in a jug. Don't boil the fruit pulp for a second time. Complete the jelly as before.

For quantity, see page 12
500g (1lb 2oz) rosehips, stalks removed
1kg (2lb 4oz) cooking or tart apples,
   roughly chopped
warmed sugar (see page 10; for quantity
   see step 2)

rosehip jelly

Though not instantly obvious, the juice from these wild berries is rich in vitamin C and has a fantastic flavour. As these fruits are stuffed full of tiny seeds and short itching hairs that are completely inedible, it is necessary to extract the juice from the hips first. This does make rosehips particularly well suited to jelly-making, as cooking them first and pouring through a jelly bag leaves all the unwanted pulp behind.

1 Place the rosehips and the apples in a preserving pan. Add enough water to cover them and simmer gently for around 45 minutes until the fruit is soft and pulpy. Mash the fruit with the back of a spoon, then pour it into a jelly bag and leave undisturbed overnight, collecting the drips underneath in a measuring jug.

2 Allow 450g (1lb) sugar to every 600ml (1 pint) juice. Place the juice in a preserving pan, add the warmed sugar and stir over a low heat until all the sugar has dissolved, then turn up the heat and boil rapidly to reach setting point (see page 10). Skim if necessary (see page 11).

3 Pour the jelly into hot, sterilized jars (see page 8) and seal (see page 11).

rowan jelly

Rowan berries come from the mountain ash tree and make a well set jelly, with their slightly bitter flavour offset by apples or quinces. Serve as an accompaniment to venison, grouse and hare.

Use equal amounts of rowan berries and apples, or quinces if you have some, for this jelly. Make it in the same way as the Rosehip Jelly. As this preserve is often served with rich meats, adding chopped rosemary to the jelly before potting works well, though it is inclined to settle at the bottom of the jars.

For quantity, see page 12
1kg (2lb 4oz) crab apples, roughly chopped
sugar (for quantity see step 4)

crab apple jelly

Crab apples seem like such a neglected fruit, yet in season they are often abundant. Their small size makes them far too fiddly for peeling and coring, so you either make them into jelly or purée the fruit for curds, fruit butters or pie fillings. When making jelly, the idea is to end up with something that is as clear as can be.

Different apples will produce jellies in different shades, from amber to rose, and they always look beautiful when the light shines through them. For a spicier version, add a few cloves, a cinnamon stick or some slices of root ginger to the fruit when it is being cooked at the beginning, though I much prefer the single flavour of the fruit to sing through.

1 Place the apples in a preserving pan with 500ml (18fl oz) water. Simmer for about 45 minutes until the fruits have softened and turned fluffy, mashing them with a wooden spoon.

2 Place the apples in a jelly bag suspended over a measuring jug to catch the drips. Allow the apples to drain naturally for several hours or overnight – don't be tempted to squeeze the bag if you want your jelly to be beautifully clear.

3 To extract more juice, remove the pulp from the bag, place in a pan with 300ml (10½fl oz) water and bring it to the boil again. Return it to the bag and allow to drain again for a few hours.

4 Allow 450g (1lb) sugar to every 600ml (1 pint) juice. Add the sugar to the juice, stirring over a low heat until the sugar has completely dissolved. Turn up the heat and boil rapidly to reach setting point (see page 10).

5 Skim if necessary (see page 11). Pour the jelly into hot, sterilized jars (see page 8) and seal (see page 11).

For quantity, see page 12
500g (1lb 2oz) apples
500g (1lb 2oz) damsons
sugar (for quantity see step 4 of Crab
    Apple Jelly)

damson & apple jelly

Making damsons into jelly is the perfect solution to the 'stoning the fruit'
dilemma – the most tedious aspect of this fruit. Let the jelly bag do the work.

Follow the instructions for Crab Apple Jelly, first cooking the
apples in 500ml (17fl oz) water and adding the damsons for
the final 15 minutes. Pour the mixed fruits into a jelly bag
and complete as before.

For quantity, see page 12
500g (1lb 2oz) apples
500g (1lb 2oz) sloes
sugar (for quantity see step 4 of Crab
    Apple Jelly)

sloe & apple jelly

Sloes added to an apple jelly give it an exquisite rosy
hue and a lovely tart taste. This is another versatile
preserve, which works with both sweet and savoury
things and can be served with meats and cheeses. Sloes
are supposed to be best picked after the first frost and
can be found by foraging in the hedgerows.

Follow the instructions for Crab Apple
Jelly, first cooking the apples in 500ml
(17fl oz) water, then adding the sloes
during the last 15 minutes of cooking
time. Pour everything into a jelly bag
and complete as before.

For quantity, see page 12
1.4kg (3lb 2oz) blackberries
juice of ½ lemon
sugar (for quantity see step 3)

bramble jelly

Children seem to love collecting blackberries, so put them to work gathering the fruit for this jelly. Often bramble jelly has added spices but I much prefer the real fruit taste to dominate so here I have opted for the pure fruit with just a hint of lemon to help it set.

1 Place the berries in a preserving pan with 100ml (3½fl oz) water. Simmer the fruit for 5 minutes until soft, mashing the berries with a wooden spoon.

2 Pour the fruit into a jelly bag, suspended over a measuring jug to catch the drips, and leave for several hours or overnight until the pulp left in the bag is almost dry.

3 Allow 450g (1lb) sugar for every 600ml (1 pint) juice. Add the lemon juice to the blackberry juice and pour into a preserving pan. Add the sugar and stir over a gentle heat until it is completely dissolved, then turn up the heat and boil rapidly to reach setting point (see page 10).

4 Skim if necessary (see page 11). Pour the jelly into hot, sterilized jars (see page 8) and seal (see page 11).

raspberry jelly

This jelly is the most wondrous, jewel-like colour and is superbly fruity, making it ideal for using as the filling in a sponge cake. It also suits anyone who hates bits and seeds in their preserves.

Follow the instructions for Bramble Jelly, substituting raspberries for the blackberries.

marmalades

'Marmalade' usually refers to a preserve made from citrus fruits, served with toast at breakfast. Bitter Seville oranges make the best traditional citrus marmalade. However, the first marmalade was made from quinces and had Portuguese origins, while in France marmalade is made from other puréed fruits.

Makes 1.3kg (3lb)
500g (1lb 2oz) blackcurrants
500g (1lb 2oz) apples, cut into large chunks
warmed sugar (see page 10; for quantity
   see step 3)

apple & blackcurrant marmalade

Although this marmalade doesn't contain any citrus fruits, the blackcurrants give just the right amount of tartness and punch to make it a perfect preserve for serving at breakfast. Processing the fruits through a food mill makes the most use of the fruit with very little preparation: there is no need to peel and core the apples at the beginning as the food mill separates these from the flesh later to leave a purée that still has some texture to it.

As is often the case, when there are apples available, there is usually an abundant supply, and this is another great way of finding a use for an apple glut. Windfalls will do the job nicely, as this recipe doesn't call for the most perfect specimens.

1 Strip the blackcurrants from their stalks by running the tines of a fork through the stems.

2 Place all the fruit together in a pan with 3 tablespoons water (just enough to keep the fruit from catching on the bottom of the pan). Simmer gently until the fruit is soft, the juices flow and the apples are fluffy. Remove from the heat and leave until cool enough to handle.

3 Press the fruit mixture through the fine disc of a food mill or a sieve into a bowl. Weigh the purée, then pour it into a preserving pan and add an equal weight of warmed sugar. Stir over a low heat until all the sugar has dissolved, then turn up the heat and boil rapidly to reach setting point (see page 10). Skim if necessary (see page 11).

4 Pour the marmalade into hot, sterilized jars (see page 8) and seal (see page 11).

apple & cranberry marmalade

This is a variation on the previous recipe and it illustrates the supreme versatility of apples and how they will blend with just about any fruit. Using this template, you can combine whatever fruits you have a plentiful supply of, half and half with apples, cook and process to a purée, then match the weight in sugar. Make this marmalade using crab apples or varieties of cooking apple with a sharp flavour and offset them with another tangy fruit.

Follow the recipe for Apple & Blackcurrant Marmalade, substituting cranberries for the blackcurrants.

Makes 2kg (4lb 8oz)
1kg (2lb 4oz) Seville oranges

1 lemon
1.5kg (3lb 5oz) sugar

seville orange marmalade

Seville oranges are available only for a short time in late winter, but they do make the best marmalade, which makes finding them worth the effort. Because of their extremely bitter taste, they are used only for cooking, but it is this robust quality that makes them particularly good when cooked and sweetened. You are either a cut-rind person or a smooth marmalade person, but shreds of perfectly cooked sweetened rind suspended in this amber jelly get my vote any day.

1 Preheat the oven to 180°C/350°F/Gas Mark 4. Place the whole fruits in a heavy, lidded casserole or a preserving pan that will fit in the oven. Pour in 1.25 litres (2¼ pints) water and bring it to simmering point on the hob.

2 Cover the pan (if using a preserving pan, make a lid from kitchen foil) and place in the oven. Poach the fruit for 2½–3 hours, by which time the skins will be soft.

3 Using a spoon, lift the fruit out of the liquid into a colander. When cool enough to handle, cut each fruit in half and scoop out the pulp with a spoon, leaving just the peel, placing the pulp, pith and pips, in a muslin bag suspended over a bowl to catch any drips. (Alternatively, use a large piece of muslin gathered into a bag and tied with string). Measure the liquid, adding any collected in the bowl under the drained pulp, and if necessary add water to make it up to 1 litre (1¾ pints).

4 Place the muslin bag in a saucepan with enough poaching liquid to cover. Bring to the boil and simmer for 15 minutes. Leave until cool enough to handle, then squeeze the bag to get as much of the liquid as possible from the pulp. Discard the bag and its contents.

5 Chop the rind into thin strips and put into a preserving pan. Add all the poaching liquid. If the mixture is cold, you can add the sugar without warming it; otherwise you will need to warm the sugar first (see page 10). Stir the sugar into the orange liquid over a low heat until completely dissolved and the liquid is clear, then boil rapidly for 15 minutes and test for setting point (see page 10).

6 Turn off the heat and leave the marmalade to stand for 15 minutes, then stir to distribute the peel. Skim if necessary (see page 11). Pour into hot, sterilized jars (see page 8) and seal (see page 11).

Makes 1.5kg (3lb 5oz)
450g (1lb) dried figs

3 lemons
1.1kg (2lb 7oz) warmed sugar (see page 10)

lemon & fig marmalade

This unusual combination is well worth trying. The lemon half-moons are left in large chunks which give a lovely candied tang to the preserve. Along with the figs, they make a great start to the day.

1 Remove the stalks from the figs and cut each into 4 chunks. Halve the lemons lengthways, then slice the halves thinly, collecting all the juice and any pips. Place the pips in a piece of muslin and tie it into a bag with string. Place the lemon slices and juice, the figs and the wrapped pips in a large bowl, cover them with 1.1 litres (2 pints) water and leave for 24 hours.

2 Pour the mixture into a pan and heat to simmering; leave simmering for 1–1½ hours until the lemon rind is soft. Leave to cool slightly and remove the pips.

3 Add the warmed sugar. Stir over a low heat, without boiling, until the sugar has completely dissolved, then bring the marmalade to a rapid boil and cook until it reaches setting point (see page 10). Skim if necessary (see page 11). Pot into hot, sterilized jars (see page 8) and seal (see page 11).

Makes 1kg (2lb 4oz)
juice and pared rind of 12 limes
680g (1½lb) warmed sugar (see page 10)

lime marmalade

If you fancy a change from traditional orange marmalade, then this is the recipe to try. Here is another useful marmalade that can be made at any time of year using shop-bought fruit. It has a great colour and flavour.

Shred the rind pieces finely. Place the pith and pips from the limes in a piece of muslin and tie it up with string. Put the lime rind and juice and 1.7 litres (3 pints) water into a preserving pan and bring to the boil, then simmer for 1 hour until the rind is soft. Add the warmed sugar and stir over a low heat until all the sugar has dissolved, then turn up the heat and boil rapidly to reach setting point (see page 10). Remove the muslin bag, then pot up.

Makes 1.3kg (3lb)
900g (2lb) peaches, roughly chopped
750g (1lb 10oz) sugar

peach marmalade

I usually choose a tangy citrus preserve to spread on my toast at breakfast, but this aromatic, slightly gentler marmalade makes a lovely start to the day. You can, of course, eat it just about any time, but it has become one of my morning favourites. The cooking brings out the superb aroma of the fruit – and you could add some vanilla for an even more sybaritic experience.

1 Place the peaches and their stones in a pan along with 250ml (9fl oz) water. Bring them to simmering point and simmer until the peach pieces are soft.

2 Discard the stones and press the flesh through the fine disc of a food mill or a sieve, to give a purée.

3 Put the purée into a preserving pan, add the sugar, warmed if necessary (see page 65) and stir gently over a low heat until the sugar has completely dissolved. Turn up the heat and boil until it reaches setting point (see page 10). Skim if necessary (see page 11).

4 Pour the marmalade into hot, sterilized jars (see page 8) and seal (see page 11).

peach & vanilla marmalade

Vanilla adds an unmistakable flavour to this breakfast classic. Peaches are wonderfully fragrant anyway, so with added vanilla become positively heavenly. The sticky black seeds scraped from the vanilla pod disperse throughout the preserve. Though called marmalade, it would be a shame to think it can only be eaten for breakfast. This one's a good all rounder.

Split a vanilla pod lengthways and add it to the peaches when cooking them with the water, as above. Remove the pod before puréeing the fruit and scrape the seeds from the pod pieces, using the sharp point of a knife. Stir the seeds into the peach purée and discard the pod pieces. Continue as above.

Makes about 1.5kg (3lb 5oz)
1kg (2lb 4oz) quinces, fur washed off
3 oranges

warmed sugar (see page 10; for quantity see step 5)

quince & orange marmalade

Reputedly, the original marmalade was a preserve made from quinces, and the name comes from the word *marmelo*, the Portuguese word for this fruit. Quince seems to be a long-forgotten fruit, not often found for sale, though you may come across it in Mediterranean food stores. If you have a quince tree, use these wonderful fruits with orange to make a delicious marmalade. The quinces are cooked very slowly to intensify their flavour and bring out the best in them – use the oven on the lowest setting or cook the marmalade in a slow cooker for a similar result.

1 Place the fruits in a lidded casserole dish (use a second casserole if they won't all fit into one) and pour in enough boiling water to cover the fruits so they just begin to float. Put on the lid and slow cook in the oven for 6–8 hours or overnight, or cook in a slow cooker or crock-pot.

2 Remove from the oven and leave until cool enough to handle. Strain the liquid through a colander into a pan. Peel the quinces, quarter them and remove the cores, then place the skins and cores in with the cooking liquid. Cut 2 of the oranges in half, scoop out the flesh and add the pips and pith to the liquid as well. Put the peel to one side.

3 Bring the mixture to the boil and reduce it down to about a third or a half of the original quantity. Pour the reduced mixture through a sieve into a preserving pan.

4 Cut the quinces into chunky slices about 2cm (¾in) square and 1cm (½in) thick. Slice the whole orange into thin rounds and chop the empty orange halves into fine shreds.

5 Weigh the quince, orange slices and shredded rind, add them to the reduced mixture and warm through. Add the same weight of warmed sugar and stir over a low heat until all the sugar has dissolved, taking care to keep the orange slices intact, then turn up the heat and boil rapidly to reach setting point (see page 10). Skim if necessary (see page 11).

6 Remove the orange slices with a slotted spoon and use them to decorate the insides of the hot, sterilized jars (see page 8) by standing them on end against the glass. Pour the marmalade into the jars and seal (see page 11).

curds

These little pots of fruity loveliness are totally delicious. I make a selection of curds and serve them in teaspoon-sized dollops in bite-sized sweet pastry cases. Each one can be savoured, discussed and relished with due ceremony. Fruit curds don't keep quite so well as jams, but they won't hang around long enough anyway.

Makes 900g (2lb)
1 vanilla pod
600g (1lb 5oz) crab apples, halved, or
cooking apples cut roughly into chunks

115g (4oz) butter, preferably unsalted,
cut into cubes
450g (1lb) caster sugar
3 large eggs plus 2 egg yolks, beaten

crab apple & vanilla curd

Crab apples have just the right amount of tartness to give this curd lots of flavour, but any sharp apples will do the job just as well. Because the fruit is puréed, there isn't much preparation needed, so windfalls can be used, if desired, more or less as they are (just with any bad bits removed). This curd makes the most fabulous filling for a sweet pastry case.

1 Split the vanilla pod lengthways and place it with the apples in a pan, adding 1 tablespoon water. Simmer gently until the apples are soft, stirring occasionally to be sure the fruit doesn't catch on the bottom of the pan. Remove it from the heat and leave to cool.

2 Remove the vanilla pod, then purée the apples by pressing them through the fine disc of a food mill or a sieve, collecting the resulting purée in a bowl. Scrape the seeds from the vanilla pod pieces with a sharp knife and add them to the apples along with the pod. Add the other ingredients, pouring the egg through a sieve.

3 Place the bowl over a pan of simmering water (or use a double boiler) and heat gently, stirring all the time until everything is blended and the curd begins to thicken and coats the back of the spoon. This stage should take about 20–30 minutes.

4 Remove the vanilla pod pieces. Pour the hot curd into small, hot, sterilized jars (see page 8) and seal (see page 11).

Makes 500g (1lb 2oz)
225g (8oz) apricots, quartered and stoned
2 eggs, well beaten
zest and juice of 1 lemon

50g (1¾oz) butter, preferably unsalted,
  cut into cubes
225g (8oz) caster sugar

apricot curd

Fresh home-grown apricots cannot be bettered, but even a punnet-full from the supermarket will make tasty curd. Choose the best quality organic eggs when making curds as they also help to give a brighter colour to the finished product.

1 Place the apricots in a pan with 2 tablespoons water (just enough to stop the fruit from catching on the bottom of the pan) and cook gently until soft.

2 Cool the fruit slightly, then press it through the fine disc of a food mill or a sieve, collecting the resulting purée in a bowl.

3 Strain the beaten eggs through a sieve into the purée. Add the lemon zest and juice, the butter and the sugar.

4 Place the bowl over a pan of simmering water (or use a double boiler). Cook gently, stirring continuously with a wooden spoon, until the mixture is completely blended and thickens enough to coat the back of the spoon. This should take about 30 minutes.

5 Pour the curd into small, hot, sterilized jars (see page 8) and seal (see page 11).

Makes 350g (12oz)
250g (9oz) raspberries
170g (6oz) caster sugar

50g (1¾oz) butter, preferably unsalted,
    cut into cubes
2 eggs, beaten

raspberry curd

Raspberries give this delicious curd a wonderful colour and a lovely tangy taste. Save small unusual-shaped glass jars especially for potting up curds. They are great to give as presents.

1 Place the raspberries in a pan and cook gently for 5–10 minutes, squashing the fruits with a spoon to help release the juice.

2 Push the fruit through a sieve, collecting the purée in a bowl.

3 Place the bowl over a pan of simmering water (or use a double boiler) and add all the other ingredients, pouring the beaten eggs through a sieve onto the purée. Stir with a wooden spoon until everything is well blended. Continue cooking, stirring constantly, until the curd is thick enough to coat the back of the spoon – this should take about 20–30 minutes.

4 Pour the curd into small, hot, sterilized jars (see page 8) and seal (see page 11).

Makes 450g (1lb)
225g (8oz) blueberries
zest and juice of 1 lime

50g (1¾oz) butter, preferably
    unsalted, cut into cubes
225g (8oz) caster sugar
2 eggs, beaten

blueberry & lime curd

The best and tastiest blueberries err on the tart side and here these berries benefit from an added boost with the addition of the zest and juice of a lime.

Place the blueberries in a pan with the lime zest and juice and cook gently for 5–10 minutes until tender. Purée the fruit and continue as for steps 2–4 of Raspberry Curd.

Makes 450g (1lb)
450g (1lb) gooseberries, any large
    stems removed
zest of 1 lime
100g (3½oz) butter, preferably unsalted,
    cut into cubes
200g (7oz) caster sugar
3 large eggs plus 2 yolks, beaten

gooseberry curd

This curd isn't one you are likely to find for sale anywhere, so you have no option but to make it yourself at home. Gooseberries are relatively easy to grow and don't need much attention to flourish so it is well worth growing some just to make this curd.

1 Place the gooseberries in a pan with 85ml (3fl oz) water and cook gently for 5–10 minutes, squashing the fruits with a spoon to help release the juice.

2 Press the fruit through the fine disc of a food mill or a sieve, to remove the skins and seeds, collecting the purée in a bowl.

3 Place the bowl over a pan of simmering water (or use a double boiler) and add all the other ingredients, pouring the beaten eggs through a sieve onto the purée. Continue stirring with a wooden spoon until everything becomes well blended and smooth and thick enough to coat the back of the spoon – this should take about 20–30 minutes.

4 Pour the curd into hot, sterilized jars (see page 8) and seal (see page 11).

Makes 400g (14oz)
zest and juice of 3 lemons
85g (3oz) butter, preferably unsalted,
cut into cubes

200g (7oz) caster sugar
3 large eggs, beaten

lemon curd

An outstanding classic, this sharp lemon curd makes the perfect filling for an open tart, can be used to sandwich a sponge cake, spread on freshly-baked bread or swirled through vanilla ice cream. Utter perfection, whichever way you serve it.

1 Place the lemon zest and juice in a bowl set over a pan of simmering water (or use a double boiler) along with the butter and sugar. Add the beaten eggs, pouring them through a sieve.

2 Stir with a wooden spoon until everything becomes heated through and well blended. Continue cooking, stirring constantly, until the curd thickens enough to coat the back of the spoon – this should take about 15–20 minutes.

3 Pour the curd into small, hot, sterilized jars (see page 8), seal (see page 11).

Makes 350g (12oz)
zest and juice of 3 Seville oranges
50g (1¾oz) butter, preferably
unsalted, cut into cubes

170g (6oz) caster sugar
2 large eggs, beaten

bitter orange curd

The bitter nature of Seville oranges works perfectly for a curd. Most sweet oranges just don't have enough character to use in this way, although blood oranges have more of a flavour kick than other sweet varieties, so they work well also. Use the curd as a filling for a sweet pastry tart, or spread it liberally to sandwich the layers of a rich chocolate cake, or simply serve it on a thick slice of fresh bread.

Follow the instructions for making Lemon Curd using the ingredients above.

Makes 400g (14oz)
zest of 2 small graperfruit
6 tbsp grapefruit juice

85g (3oz) butter, preferably
unsalted, cut into cubes
200g (7oz) caster sugar
3 large eggs, beaten

grapefruit curd

Here's another citrus variation on the lemon curd theme. This curd is smooth and creamy but still has its own distinct tang.

Follow the instructions for making Lemon Curd using the ingredients above.

Makes 1.4kg (3lb)
1 small butternut squash, peeled,
    deseeded and roughly chopped
zest and juice of 1 lemon
zest and juice of 1 orange
70g (2½oz) butter, preferably unsalted,
    cut into cubes
200g (7oz) caster sugar
2 large eggs plus 2 yolks, beaten
4 pieces of stem ginger (about 75g/2¾oz),
    finely chopped
3 tbsp syrup from the stem ginger

butternut & ginger curd

Squashes and pumpkins are naturally sweet so can be made into sweet preserves really well. Here butternut squash is the main ingredient, but other types can be used instead. The brighter orange the flesh, the better. Chopped pieces of stem ginger add a lovely bite to the texture.

1 Place the squash in a pan with 100ml (3½fl oz) water to stop it from sticking to the pan as it cooks. Cover and cook until soft, then pour off any excess liquid.

2 Purée the squash in a food processor or pass it through the fine disc of a food mill. Alternatively, press it through a sieve.

3 Measure out 300g (10½oz) of the squash purée and place this in a bowl over simmering water (or use a double boiler), along with all the other ingredients, pouring the beaten eggs through a sieve onto the purée. Continue stirring with a wooden spoon until everything becomes well blended, the sugar is dissolved and the curd thickens and will coat the back of the spoon – this should take about 30 minutes.

4 Pour the curd into small, hot, sterilized jars (see page 8) and seal (see page 11).

cordials

Cordials and syrups are, in fact, the same thing. These sweetened fruity concentrates are delicious diluted with water, added to milk for milk shakes, poured over ice cream or swirled through cake mixture prior to baking for a marbled effect. At best they really capture the essence of the fruit. Use over-ripe fruit for best results.

Makes about 750ml (1¼ pints)
900g (2lb) over-ripe blackcurrants
sugar (for quantity see step 3)

blackcurrant cordial

Rich in vitamin C, blackcurrants are an ideal fruit for making into cordials that can then be diluted either as a cold drink or a hot comforting drink. The homemade version knocks spots off anything you will find for sale.

1 Strip the blackcurrants from their stalks by running the tines of a fork through the stems.

2 Place them with 400ml (14fl oz) water in the top of a double boiler or in a bowl over a pan of simmering water and cook for half an hour, stirring occasionally and mashing the fruit with the back of the spoon, then strain through a sieve into a measuring jug and discard the pulp.

3 Add 450g (1lb) sugar to every 600ml (1 pint) juice and stir over a low heat until all the sugar has dissolved. Bring just to the boil, then remove quickly from the heat.

4 Pour the cordial into clean clip-top or corked bottles and sterilize (see page 14), or pour into freezer containers, seal and freeze.

damson cordial

Made into a cordial, freshly picked damsons make a sublime and unusual cordial bursting with tart flavour. Drizzle over yogurt or ice cream.

Follow the recipe for Blackcurrant Cordial, substituting damsons for the blackcurrants.

Makes about 1.5 litres (2½ pints)
20 heads of elderflower
1.5kg (3lb 5oz) sugar
40g (1½oz) citric acid
2 lemons, thinly sliced
2 oranges, thinly sliced

elderflower cordial

The shrubby elder (*Sambucus nigra*) is so common in the countryside that it is easy to pass it by without a second look. Yet in early summer it provides one of the most distinctive ingredients of the preserving year – one that can be foraged for free. The heavily scented blossoms make a refreshing cordial that you can dilute with still or sparkling mineral water. The fragrance, as well as the taste, evokes lazy summer afternoons. Gather the flower heads on dry, sunny days, away from busy roads, and select flower heads that are fresh and white, avoiding older creamy-yellow blossoms. This delicious cordial will keep for around 2 months in the fridge; if frozen in plastic containers, it will last for a year or more – so be sure to make plenty.

1 Shake the flowers, face down, to remove any unwanted creatures.

2 Place the sugar and 1.2 litres (2¼ pints) water in a stainless steel or enamel pan and warm slowly, stirring, to dissolve the sugar completely, then bring the resulting syrup to a boil.

3 Add the flowers, bring again to the boil, then remove from the heat.

4 Add the other ingredients, stir well, then leave, covered, in a cool place for 24 hours.

5 Strain the cordial into clean clip-top or corked bottles and sterilize (see page 14).

Makes about 750ml (1¼ pints)
50g (2oz) fresh root ginger, bruised

juice and thinly pared rind of 2 lemons
sugar (for quantity see step 2)

ginger & lemon cordial

This cordial, though not intentionally medicinal, is soothing and warming and is ideal to drink as a hot beverage if you feel a cold coming on.

1 Place the ginger and and lemon rind in a pan with 1.2 litres (2¼ pints) water. Simmer gently for 40 minutes. Strain through a sieve into a measuring jug and discard the rind and ginger.

2 Add 400g (14oz) sugar to every 600ml (1 pint) liquid and the lemon juice and stir over a low heat until all the sugar has dissolved. Bring just to the boil, then remove quickly from the heat.

3 Pour the cordial into clean clip-top or corked bottles and sterilize (see page 14), or pour into freezer containers, seal and freeze.

Makes about 2 litres (3½ pints)
8–10 lemons
6–8 oranges

650g (1lb 7oz) sugar
1½ tsp citric acid

lemon & orange cordial

A fresh citrus cordial that is so classic and versatile that you can drink it any time. This cordial makes a drink like the best old-fashioned lemonade mixed with orangeade.

Pare the rind finely from 1 lemon and 1 orange. Put the sugar, rind and 600ml (1 pint) water into a pan. Heat gently to make a syrup, then boil for 5 minutes. Strain through a sieve into a measuring jug; discard the rind. Squeeze sufficient lemons and oranges to produce the same amount of juice as syrup, keeping the proportions half lemon, half orange. Mix the syrup and fruit juices together in the pan and add the citric acid, stirring until the powder has dissolved. Bottle as above.

Makes 600ml (1 pint)
450g (1lb) rosehips, freshly gathered
sugar (for quantity see step 5)

rosehip cordial

Rosehips are one of the most popular foraged fruits, offered for free from nature's larder. They are the fruit of the wild rose, and gathering them is all part of the fun. They should be picked fully ripe, when a deep red colour and preferably after the first frosts, which soften them. If picked a little earlier, you can place them, freshly picked, into the freezer overnight to give the same result as if they had been nipped by the frost. Rosehip cordial has a high vitamin C content and is so sweet and delicious that it is a great way of encouraging children to boost their vitamin intake effortlessly.

1 Place the rosehips in a pan and mash them with the back of a spoon to break them down. Pour 1 litre (1¾ pints) boiling water over them, to cover, and simmer for 5 minutes until the hips are soft.

2 Remove the pan from the heat and leave to stand for 15 minutes, then strain the mixture through a jelly bag, collecting the juice in a measuring jug. Set the juice aside.

3 Remove the pulp from the jelly bag and place it in the pan. Add 500ml (17fl oz) water and bring the mixture to the boil, then repeat step 2, but this time squeezing out the excess liquid from the pulp.

4 Combine both jugs of juice in the pan and boil the mixture to reduce it by approximately a third to a half.

5 Add 325g (11½oz) sugar to every 600ml (1 pint) juice and stir over a low heat until all the sugar has dissolved. Bring just to the boil, then remove quickly from the heat.

6 Pour the cordial into clean clip-top or corked bottles and sterilize (see page 14), or pour into freezer containers, seal and freeze.

Makes about 600ml (1 pint)
1kg (2lb 4oz) over-ripe raspberries
sugar (for quantity see step 2)

raspberry cordial

Raspberry cordial makes a lovely alternative to a dollop of jam on your rice pudding. Unlike preserves, which often benefit from being made with combinations and medleys of flavours, cordials are usually best when made with a single fruit, thus showcasing the individual characteristics of that fruit.

1 Place the raspberries and in the top of a double boiler or in a bowl over a pan of simmering water. Mash the berries with the back of a spoon to break them down and add 1 tablespoon water, then cook until the fruit is soft, the juices are flowing and the fruit comes to the boil, stirring now and again. Pour into a jelly bag and collect the drips in a measuring jug.

2 Add 400g (14oz) sugar to every 600ml (1 pint) juice and stir over a low heat until all the sugar has dissolved. Bring just to the boil, then remove quickly from the heat.

3 Pour the cordial into clean clip-top or corked bottles and sterilize (see page 14), or pour into freezer containers, seal and freeze.

Makes about 1.2 litres (2¼ pints)
600g (1lb 5oz) sugar

1kg (2lb 4oz) over-ripe apricots, halved and stoned

apricot cordial

Another lush and fruity treat to dilute down into a refreshing summer drink. It is still worth making a smaller quantity even if there aren't many apricots to go around.

Put the sugar and 1.2 litres (2¼ pints) water in a pan and heat gently to make a syrup. Add the apricots to the syrup, simmering until the fruit pieces are tender. Strain through a sieve into a measuring jug. (Do not discard the apricots. Instead, use them as a delicious pie filling or serve them with cream.) Pour the cordial into clean clip-top or corked bottles and sterilize (see page 14), or pour into freezer containers, seal and freeze.

strawberry cordial

The vibrant colour and evocative scent of this syrup shouts out summer. Pick your own or choose locally-grown fruit so the berries are at their freshest and sweetest.

Follow the recipe for Raspberry Cordial, substituting strawberries for the raspberries.

Makes about 600ml (1 pint)
900g (2lb) over-ripe blackberries
sugar (for quantity see step 2)

blackberry cordial

An unusual twist for this foraged fruit when topped up with a sparkling white wine or a glug of champagne to make a kir royale with a rustic kick.

1 Place the blackberries with 100ml (3½fl oz) water in the top of a double boiler or in a bowl over a pan of simmering water. Cook for 1 hour, stirring occasionally and mashing the fruit with the back of the spoon, then strain through a sieve into a measuring jug and discard the pulp.

2 Add 450g (1lb) sugar to every 600ml (1 pint) juice and stir over a low heat until all the sugar has dissolved. Bring just to the boil, then remove quickly from the heat.

3 Pour the cordial into clean clip-top or corked bottles and sterilize (see page 14), or pour into freezer containers, seal and freeze.

Makes about 600ml (1 pint)
1kg (2lb 4oz) over-ripe mulberries
sugar (for quantity see below)

mulberry cordial

Gathering mulberries can be a hazardous occupation. The traditional method involves spreading a sheet on the ground underneath the branches and shaking the tree until the fruit drops.

Place the mulberries in the top of a double boiler or in a bowl over a pan of simmering water. Mash the fruits with the back of a spoon to break them down and add 1 tablespoon water, then cook until the fruit is soft and the juices are flowing and the fruit comes to the boil, stirring now and again. Pour into a jelly bag and collect the drips in a measuring jug. Add 400g (14oz) sugar to every 600ml (1 pint) juice and stir over a low heat until all the sugar has dissolved. Bring just to the boil, then remove quickly from the heat. Bottle as above.

Makes about 600ml (1 pint)
700g (1lb 9oz) over-ripe redcurrants
3 over-ripe nectarines (approx. 450g/1lb
   in weight), halved, stoned and diced
sugar (for quantity see step 3)

redcurrant & nectarine cordial

Redcurrants and nectarines make a colourful cordial that tastes great as well. As is the way with all cordials, you could pour this into ice-lolly moulds and freeze.

1 Strip the redcurrants from their stalks – the simplest and quickest way is to run the tines of a fork through the stems.

2 Place the nectarines in the top of a double boiler or in a bowl over a pan of simmering water. Mash the fruits with the back of a spoon to break them down and add 100ml (3fl oz) water. Cook until the fruit is soft, then add the redcurrants and continue to cook until they are soft and the juice is flowing. Strain through a sieve into a measuring jug and discard the pulp.

3 Add 400g (14oz) sugar to every 600ml (1 pint) juice and stir over a low heat until all the sugar has dissolved. Bring just to the boil, then remove quickly from the heat.

4 Pour the cordial into clean clip-top or corked bottles and sterilize (see page 14), or pour into freezer containers, seal and freeze.

fruits in syrup

Before the advent of the freezer, bottling fruits and vegetables in water or sugar syrup was the usual way to preserve them. Now that bottling has become a niche activity and freezing the norm, fruits in syrup have taken on an altogether more luxurious feel. Packed in smart jars and spiced or flavoured, they make brilliant presents.

Makes 750ml (1¼ pints)
450g (1lb) sugar
pared rind and juice of 1 orange
1 small cinnamon stick

4 cardamom pods, with seeds crushed
2 star anise
750g (1lb 10oz) apricots, halved and stoned

apricots in syrup

This is a lovely way of using up any luscious apricots that come your way. The syrup is quite spicy and helps make this bottled fruit very special, special enough to serve alone as dessert after dinner. Leaving the whole spices in the jar means it looks good as well.

1 Make a syrup by placing 600ml (1 pint) water in a pan with the sugar, 3 strips of the orange rind plus the juice of the orange and the spices. Heat gently, stirring to dissolve the sugar before turning up the heat and bringing to a simmer.

2 Add the apricots and poach them until they are cooked but still in whole pieces, then remove them with a slotted spoon and pack them into hot, sterilized jars (see page 8). Bring the syrup to the boil and boil rapidly for 10–15 minutes to thicken and reduce the syrup.

3 Pour the syrup and spices over the fruit to cover completely. Gently tap the jars to release any air bubbles, then seal.

nectarines in syrup

Using just a single pack of fruit to fill a jar with preserved nectarines will be a special treat to look forward to, ready for opening sometime later.

Use 750g (1lb 10oz) nectarines in place of the apricots in Apricots in Syrup. Medium-sized fruits can be used halved with the stones removed, but for larger fruits cut them into quarters and proceed as before.

damsons in syrup

As the damsons are kept whole, you might like to warn anyone eating them to beware of the stones. It is a small price to pay and you can always play tinker, tailor, soldier, sailor with the stones.

Use damsons in place of apricots, but keep the fruits whole and poach them gently in the syrup, removing them as soon as you see signs of the skins splitting. Damsons almost always have such a superb flavour that too many spices will only spoil them, so, keep the orange peel and juice but omit the spices from Apricots in Syrup. A darker sugar will also suit this fruit, so use demerara or dark muscovado instead of white sugar.

Fills a 500ml (17fl oz) jar
50g (2oz) sugar
½ vanilla pod

3cm (1¼in) piece of cinnamon stick
6–7 figs, halved
¼ tsp citric acid

figs in vanilla syrup

These gorgeous fruits look magnificent in the jar, beautifully pink and jewel-like. Baking the jar in the oven will help the figs to keep.

1 Preheat the oven to 150°C (300°F) Gas Mark 2. Place the sugar, vanilla pod and cinnamon stick in a pan and add 220ml (7½fl oz) water. Stir over a low heat to dissolve the sugar, then bring to the boil and simmer for 2 minutes to make a syrup. Remove from the heat. Discard the cinnamon stick. Slice the vanilla pod in half lengthways, scrape out the seeds with a knife and add them to the syrup.

2 Pack the figs into a clean sterilized jar (see page 8) with the cut sides facing outwards. Push the vanilla pod halves among the figs. Pour the syrup over the figs to fill the jar, swivelling the jar to remove any air bubbles.

3 Wrap kitchen foil over the top of the jar and place it in the oven, on a baking tray lined with several layers of folded newspaper. Bake for 25–30 minutes, by which time the syrup will have turned a lovely shade of pink. Remove from the oven, discard the foil and seal.

Makes 1 litre (1¾ pints)
6 oranges, cut into 5mm (¼in) slices
400ml (14fl oz) white wine vinegar
300g (10oz) sugar

120g (4oz) clear pale honey
1 small cinnamon stick
2 tsp whole coriander seeds
1 tsp whole cloves

orange slices in spiced honey

Using a medley of spices to flavour and honey to sweeten makes a delicious and aromatic syrup.

Place the orange slices in a pan with just enough water to cover. Bring to the boil and simmer for 1 hour until the rind is tender. Strain off the water and discard. Place all other ingredients in a pan and heat gently, stirring, to dissolve the sugar and honey. Add the orange slices and simmer for 30 minutes until the rind is translucent, then pack the slices into sterilized jars (see page 8). Strain the syrup to remove the spices, then return to the pan and boil rapidly for a further 10 minutes to reduce. Pour into the jars to the brim, then seal.

Fills a 1kg (2lb 4oz) wide-necked jar
900g (2lb) small peaches (approx. 9 peaches)
300g (10oz) sugar
1 vanilla pod (optional)
about 250ml (9fl oz) brandy

whole peaches in brandy

Preserving peaches in a brandy syrup is a great way to use up peaches being sold off cheaply at the supermarket. Quite often you find them still firm and perfect, but the date on the packaging turns them into a bargain. Of course if you grow your own peaches, even better! Packed into a jar, they make a wonderful present that looks very impressive. Including a vanilla pod is optional, but it is a resourceful way of using up pods that have already had their seeds removed for other recipes, and they look good showing through the jar. This recipe makes enough to fill one big jar, so adapt quantities if you want to use smaller jars.

1 Skin the peaches by plunging them in boiling water for a couple of minutes. You may need to do this in batches. The skins should peel away easily from the fruits using a sharp knife.

2 Place 400ml (14fl oz) water in a pan with half of the sugar and stir over a low heat to dissolve the sugar. Bring the syrup to a simmer and add the vanilla pod, if using.

3 Add the skinned peaches to the syrup, probably in 3 batches, and poach for 5 minutes, spooning the syrup over them if it doesn't cover them. Remove with a slotted spoon and place in a clean sterilized jar, packing them in neatly but taking care not to squash or damage them. Remove the pod from the syrup and push it down among the fruits.

4 Add the remaining sugar to the syrup in the pan and stir until all the sugar has dissolved, then turn up the heat and boil rapidly for 4 minutes. Remove from the heat and leave to cool for 10 minutes.

5 Measure the syrup, add the same amount of brandy and stir together. Pour the brandy syrup over the peaches to cover, then seal the jar.

greengages in brandy

The greengages have a great colour and aromatic flavour that works really well here. Any brandy left over in the jar after dishing up the fruit can be drunk like a liqueur. Don't waste a drop!

Follow the recipe for Whole Peaches in Brandy, substituting 900g (2lb) of firm, ripe greengages for the peaches. There is no need to skin the greengages. Be careful when poaching the fruits that they stay whole, and remove them immediately from the syrup if they show signs of splitting.

Makes about 750ml (1¼ pints)
450g (1lb) ripe cherries
75g (2¾oz) sugar
500ml (17fl oz) eau de vie

cherries in eau de vie

This has to be the easiest preserve in the book and yet very little effort is rewarded with such a luxurious result. Serve simply with cream and enjoy.

1 Use a cherry stoner to pit the cherries and remove any stalks, then pack them into sterilized, wide-necked jars (see page 8), layering the fruits with sugar now and again. When the jars are filled with cherries, spoon any remaining sugar on top.

2 Pour the eau de vie over the cherries, filling the jars to the top, and seal. Store the jars for at least 6 weeks, giving the jars a shake from time to time to help dissolve the sugar and create a syrup.

chutneys

Chutney making is an inexact science, and you can adjust spices and sweetness to suit your tastes. It requires a long cooking time to reach a rich, thick constituency, but don't cook it until too dry as it will dry out slightly in storage – a shiny, moist chutney is what you are aiming for. You must be patient and leave chutneys to mature.

Makes 1.3kg (3lb)

1 tsp allspice
1 tsp mustard seeds
1 tsp ground coriander
1 small cinnamon stick
450g (1lb) apricots, quartered and stoned
450g (1lb) cooking apples, peeled, cored and chopped into large chunks
750ml (1¼ pints) cider, wine or white malt vinegar

225g (8oz) sultanas, chopped
2 cloves of garlic, peeled and chopped
rind and juice of 1 lemon
1 tsp salt
2cm (¾in) square piece of fresh root ginger, peeled and finely chopped
450g (1lb) warmed sugar (see page 10)

apricot chutney

This chutney can be made using either fresh or dried fruit. Here, the recipe uses fresh apricots, making the most of a seasonal glut. However, if you want to make it out of season, you can use dried apricots instead: simply replace the fresh apricots with 300g (10oz) dried apricots, soaked for a few hours in the vinegar, then proceed in the same way.

1 Place the spices in a piece of muslin and tie it into a bag with string. Place the apricots, apples, vinegar and spice bag in a stainless steel preserving pan and bring to the boil, then simmer for 10 minutes.

2 Add the other ingredients and stir over a low heat until all the sugar has dissolved, then bring to the boil and simmer for approximately 1½ hours until the chutney is thick but still juicy, stirring occasionally.

3 Remove the muslin bag, then pour the chutney into hot, sterilized jars (see page 8) and seal (see page 11).

apricot & orange chutney

Orange is a great companion to apricots and helps the chutney to be even more colourful. This recipe is another useful one as it can be made at any time of year using dried apricots.

Replace the lemon from Apricot Chutney with 3 large oranges. Grate the zest from them and cut away and discard the white pith, then chop the orange flesh roughly. Add them in step 2 and continue as before.

Makes about 2.75kg (6lb)

900g (2lb) raw beetroot, peeled and
  coarsely grated
450g (1lb) onions, peeled and chopped
700g (1lb 9oz) cooking apples, peeled,
  cored and chopped

450g (1lb) seedless raisins
1.1 litres (2 pints) malt vinegar or spiced
  pickling vinegar (see page 13)
900g (2lb) sugar
2 tsp ground ginger

beetroot chutney

Beetroots are another vegetable that at the height of the season you either
have none of or far too many, so chutney-making suits them well.

1 Place everything in a stainless steel preserving pan and stir over a gentle
heat to dissolve the sugar. Bring to the boil, then simmer gently for about
1 hour until the beetroot and onions are soft and the chutney is thick but
still juicy, stirring occasionally.

2 Pour the chutney into hot, sterilized jars (see page 8) and seal (see page 11).

Makes 1.5kg (3lb 5oz)

400g (14oz) courgettes
2 tsp salt, plus extra for sprinkling
400g (14oz) runner beans, cut into 2cm
  (¾in) pieces
200g (7oz) sweetcorn kernels
450g (1lb) onions, finely chopped

600ml (1 pint) malt or cider vinegar
1 tbsp cornflour
1 tbsp English mustard powder
1 tbsp turmeric
1 green chilli, deseeded and finely chopped
350g (12oz) warmed demerara sugar (see
  page 10)

allotment chutney

This chutney is a great way of using up homegrown odds and ends, especially useful when
produce is growing faster than you can consume it. Try other combinations of vegetables too.

Cut the courgettes in half lengthways, then into slices. Place in a bowl and
sprinkle with salt, leave for 1 hour, then rinse the courgettes thoroughly and drain.
Place all the vegetables and the vinegar in a stainless steel preserving pan. Bring
to the boil, then simmer for 10 minutes. Mix the cornflour, mustard and turmeric
in a bowl with a few spoonfuls of vinegar from the pan to form a smooth paste.
Add the paste to the pan with the chilli and warmed sugar and stir over a low
heat until the sugar has dissolved, then simmer for ¾–1 hour until the chutney
is thick but juicy, stirring occasionally. Pot as above.

Makes 2kg (4lb 8oz)
1kg (2lb 4oz) damsons
1 litre (1¾ pints) malt vinegar
1 cinnamon stick
20g (¾oz) allspice
1 tsp cloves
300g (10½oz) cooking apples, peeled, cored and chopped

2 onions, peeled and finely chopped
250g (9oz) raisins
250g (9oz) dates, chopped
700g (1lb 9oz) soft brown sugar
2 cloves of garlic, peeled and crushed
20g (¾oz) ground ginger
1 tbsp sea salt

damson chutney

This chutney is rich, dark and heavenly. Damsons are one of my absolute favourite fruits for preserving and lend a superb flavour across the board to any jam, jelly, chutney or pickle that uses them. Removing the stones is a laborious job but is always worth the time. My chosen technique is to cook the fruits first, then remove the stones by hand (usually with the pan on my lap in front of the television). This tedious task has now become part of the chutney-making tradition for me, and since damsons have only a short season once a year, it isn't such a hardship.

1 Place the damsons in a pan with 250ml (9fl oz) of the vinegar and cook them until they are soft and bursting. Leave until cool enough to handle, then remove the stones. Place the spices in a piece of muslin and tie it into a bag with string.

2 Place all the ingredients in a stainless steel preserving pan and bring to the boil, then simmer gently for 2–2½ hours until the chutney is dark and thick but still juicy, stirring from time to time.

3 Remove the muslin bag, then pour the chutney into hot, sterilized jars (see page 8) and seal (see page 11).

Makes 1.75kg (3lb 14oz)

1kg (2lb 4oz) green tomatoes
250g (9oz) cooking apples, peeled
    and cored
450g (1lb) red onions, roughly chopped
200g (7oz) soft brown sugar
600ml (1 pint) malt vinegar

½ tsp mustard seeds
½ tsp cayenne pepper
1 tbsp finely grated fresh root ginger
200g (7oz) raisins
3 green chillies, deseeded and
    finely chopped
1 tsp salt

green tomato & red onion chutney

At the end of the season, when there is no more heat left outside to ripen the last of the tomatoes, it is time to bring them into the house. If you place them on any empty windowsill you can find, there's a chance that the last precious fruits will slowly turn from green to red. Packing them in boxes, spaced apart in layers with straw or woollen material between them, is another way of ripening them gradually and prolonging the season; but if you have plenty to spare, the still-green ones are just perfect for turning into chutney.

1 To skin the tomatoes place them in a bowl and pour boiling water over them, then leave for a minute or two. The skins should now slide off the fruits when you cut into them with a sharp knife. It is harder to remove the skins when tomatoes are green, so steeping them for longer than usual helps. Chop the tomatoes roughly.

2 Place all the ingredients in a stainless steel preserving pan and bring to the boil. Reduce the heat and simmer until everything is cooked and the chutney has thickened, stirring occasionally.

3 Pour the chutney into hot, sterilized jars (see page 8) and seal (see page 11).

Makes 1.7kg (3lb 12oz)
1.9kg (4lb 3oz) mangoes (5 or 6 medium
    fruits), skinned and stoned
2 tsp mixed pickling spices
juice and thickly pared ring of 1 orange
350g (12oz) onions, finely chopped

300ml (10½fl oz) white wine vinegar
2 cloves of garlic
1 tbsp grated root ginger
2 hot red chillies, deseeded and
    finely chopped
550g (1lb 4oz) warmed light muscovado
    sugar (see page 10)

mango chutney

A classic accompaniment with Indian food, you can't beat this sticky sweet chutney. This is a
great way of using mangoes when slightly under ripe, if, like me, you aren't ever quite sure
whether your mangoes are ripe enough to eat.

1 Cut half of the mango flesh into small pieces and leave the other half in larger
chunks. Put the pickling spices and rind pieces in a piece of muslin and tie it
into a bag.

2 Place all the ingredients except the sugar and large mango chunks in a
stainless steel preserving pan and simmer gently for 20 minutes until the mango
and onions are soft.

3 Add the rest of the mango and
simmer gently for another 5 minutes.
Add the warmed sugar and stir over
a low heat until it has completely
dissolved, then boil until the mixture
reaches a thick, jam-like consistency,
stirring gently and taking care to
retain the chunky texture.

4 Remove the muslin bag. Allow
the chutney to cool for 10 minutes,
then stir again to redistribute the bits.

5 Pour the chutney into hot,
sterilized jars (see page 8) and seal
(see page 11).

Makes 1.7kg (3lb 12oz)
1kg (2lb 4oz) nectarines, skinned, stoned
  and roughly chopped
225g (8oz) cooking apples, peeled, cored
  and chopped
225g (8oz) onions, peeled and finely sliced
225g (8oz) raisins
350g (12oz) light brown sugar
50g (2oz) stem ginger, finely chopped
2 cloves of garlic
2 tsp sea salt
1 tsp cayenne pepper
500ml (17fl oz) white wine vinegar

nectarine chutney

Nectarines work so well here. They have just the right amount of sweetness and tartness to make an excellent chutney and this one's a real favourite of mine. I like it with macaroni cheese or put in a sandwich with just about anything!

1 Place all the ingredients in a stainless steel preserving pan and stir over a gentle heat to dissolve the sugar. Simmer gently for approximately 1½ hours until the chutney is thick but still juicy, stirring occasionally.

2 Pour the chutney into hot, sterilized jars (see page 8) and seal (see page 11).

peach chutney

Peaches make a straight and worthy substitute here when used instead of nectarines. Use whichever you have in plentiful supply and you won't be disappointed.

Follow the recipe for Nectarine Chutney, substituting peaches for the nectarines. Choose fruits that are firm and only just ripened.

Makes 1.25kg (2lb 12oz)

1kg (2lb 4oz) onions, peeled and
  finely sliced
2 tbsp olive oil
500ml (17fl oz) red wine vinegar
  (or a mixture of red vine vinegar
  and balsamic vinegar)
750g (1lb 10oz) muscovado sugar
2 bay leaves
15–20 black peppercorns, crushed
2 tsp salt

onion marmalade

Really a chutney or relish, not a marmalade at all. Onion marmalade has become very fashionable in recent years, favoured by chefs and gastro-pubs alike. Generally it isn't a great keeper but this particular version, like other chutneys, will keep well.

1 Separate the onion slices into rings. Heat the oil in a stainless steel preserving pan, add the onion rings and cook them gently for about 20 minutes until they are soft but not browned.

2 Add all the other ingredients and simmer gently for 1–1½ hours until the marmalade is dark and thick but still juicy, stirring occasionally.

3 Pour the marmalade into hot, sterilized jars (see page 8) and seal (see page 11).

Makes 2kg (4lb 8oz)

1 tsp whole allspice
1 tsp coriander seeds
2 tsp mustard seeds
½ tsp cumin seeds
50g (2oz) fresh root ginger, bruised
1.5kg (3lb 5oz) red tomatoes, skinned
    and chopped
500g (1lb 2oz) cooking apples, peeled,
    cored and diced

500g (1lb 2oz) onions, peeled and finely
    chopped
2 cloves of garlic, peeled and finely chopped
250ml (9fl oz) red wine vinegar
1 tsp sea salt
200g (7oz) warmed muscovado sugar
    (see page 10)

red tomato & garlic chutney

This is another easy classic that uses up a glut of tomatoes. In fact, chutney is so easy to make that it is surprising that anyone ever buys the shop-bought stuff. Here, the red fruits and brown sugar give the chutney a lovely rich colour.

1 Place the whole spices and bruised ginger in a piece of muslin and tie it into a bag with string.

2 Place all the ingredients except the sugar in a stainless steel preserving pan and bring to the boil, then simmer until tender. Add the warmed sugar and stir over a low heat until all the sugar has dissolved. Turn up the heat and bring to the boil, then simmer gently for approximately 1½ hours until the chutney is thick but still juicy, stirring occasionally.

3 Remove the muslin bag, then pour the chutney into hot, sterilized jars (see page 8) and seal (see page 11).

hot tomato, apple & chilli chutney

As a variation on the previous recipe this version packs a punch with added oomph supplied by red hot chillies and a few extra spices – delicious. Add a dollop to pasta.

For a hot tomato chutney with a chili kick, follow Red Tomato and Garlic Chutney, adding 3 or 4 deseeded and finely chopped hot red chilies, and include 6 whole cardamom seeds with the spices and an extra couple of garlic cloves if you wish.

Makes 1.8kg (4lb)
900g (2lb) apples, peeled and cored
600ml (1 pint) cider vinegar or malt vinegar
55g (2oz) pickling spice
5g (¼oz) ground ginger
225g (8oz) raisins

450g (1lb) warmed brown sugar
  (see page 10)
2 tsp salt
1 red chilli, deseeded and finely
  chopped (optional)

aunt edna's apple chutney

I was given this recipe in the 1970s by a friend's aunt and it was the first chutney I ever made. The results are totally reliable and since then I've made it many times. Thanks Auntie Edna.

1 Place the apples and vinegar in a stainless steel preserving pan. Tie the pickling spice and ground ginger into a piece of muslin with string and add to the pan. Cook gently until the apples are tender but still hold their shape.

2 Mince the raisins in a food processor, or chop roughly, and add them to the pan with the sugar, salt and optional chilli; mix well. Bring the chutney to the boil, then remove from heat. Remove the spice bundle.

3 Pour the chutney into hot, sterilized jars (see page 8) and seal (see page 11).

Makes 1.7kg (3lb 12oz)
1kg (2lb 4oz) cooking apples, peeled,
  cored and chopped
1.2 litres (2¼ pints) malt vinegar
250g (9oz) onions, peeled and chopped

10g (¼oz) mustard seeds
1 tsp ground ginger
350g (12oz) warmed brown sugar (see
  page 10)
350g (12oz) chopped dried dates
1 clove of garlic, peeled and chopped

apple & date chutney

Every autumn I end up with bags of apples even though I only possess one small crab apple tree. Friends always have more fruit than they can cope with so another recipe to use them up is great.

Place the first 5 ingredients in a stainless steel preserving pan and stir over a gentle heat to dissolve the sugar. Bring to the boil, then simmer gently until the apples are soft. Remove from the heat and stir in the warmed sugar, dates and garlic. Return to the heat and continue cooking until the chutney is thick but still juicy, stirring occasionally. Pot up as above.

Makes 2kg (4lb 6oz)

12 peppercorns

2 tsp whole allspice

2cm (¾in) square piece of fresh root ginger, bruised

750g (1lb 10oz) pumpkin, peeled, deseeded and cut into chunks

450g (1lb) cooking apples, peeled, cored and finely chopped

50g (2oz) finely chopped stem ginger

350g (12oz) shallots, peeled, cored and finely chopped

200g (7oz) sultanas, chopped

2 cloves of garlic, finely chopped

2 tsp salt

600ml (1 pint) malt or cider vinegar

400g (14oz) warmed soft brown sugar (see page 10)

pumpkin chutney

With their wonderful shapes, textures and vibrant colours, pumpkins and squashes are always so visually appealing and their flesh gives this chutney a colourful look and sweeter flavour – always a good thing.

1 Place the dry spices and root ginger in a piece of muslin and tie it into a bag with string. Place all the ingredients except the sugar in a stainless steel preserving pan and bring slowly to the boil, then simmer gently for 20 minutes until the pumpkin and apple are soft.

2 Add the warmed sugar and stir over a gentle heat until all the sugar has dissolved, then turn up the heat and simmer for approximately 1–1½ hours until the chutney is thick but still juicy, stirring occasionally.

3 Remove the muslin bag, then pour the chutney into hot, sterilized jars (see page 8) and seal (see page 11).

marrow chutney

It is great to find 'good ways with marrows', as people who grow them always seem to end up with a glut of ginormous specimens but without a clue what to do with them. When it comes to preserving, and to chutneys in particular, marrows are a really useful 'filler-outer', in the same way that apples are. However, they are a very watery vegetable, so you need to remove some of this liquid right at the start to concentrate the flavour.

Substitute 750g (1lb 10oz) marrow for the pumpkin in Pumpkin Chutney. There is no need to add the stem ginger. Place the marrow in a bowl, sprinkle with some salt and leave for 12 hours to draw out the excess water, then rinse thoroughly and drain, then follow the recipe above.

Makes 1.7kg (3lb 12oz)

1.3kg (3lb) pears, peeled, cored and cut
    into chunks
450g (1lb) onions, peeled and chopped
grated rind and juice of 1 lemon
grated rind and juice of 1 orange
225g (8oz) sugar
225g (8oz) seedless raisins
300ml (½ pint) malt or cider vinegar
1 tsp salt
1 tsp ground ginger
½ tsp cloves

pear chutney

This chutney contains just the right combination of fruitiness and spiciness. I would always recommend that you leave chutney in the larder for a couple of months before eating it and though this pear chutney is no exception, it does taste remarkably good as soon as it is made. Keep it for a while if you can, otherwise devour and enjoy! It is great with cheese.

1 Place all the ingredients in a stainless steel preserving pan and stir over a gentle heat until all the sugar has dissolved. Bring to the boil, then simmer for approximately 2 hours until the chutney is dark and thick but still juicy, stirring occasionally. As with all chutneys, it will thicken up slightly as it cools.

2 Pour the chutney into hot, sterilized jars (see page 8) and seal (see page 11).

pickles

When it comes to pickles, vinegar is the star ingredient. Vinegar comes into its own here and the more matured and spiced it is, the better. You can use any kind of vinegar but cider vinegar goes well with apples and pears, malt vinegar with darker pickles and white wine vinegar helps the colour of ingredients to be seen at their best.

Makes about 800g (1lb 12oz)
1kg (2lb 4oz) crab apples
750ml (1¼ pints) cider or wine vinegar
1 small cinnamon stick

10 cloves
1 tsp allspice
800g (1lb 12oz) warmed sugar
  (see page 10)

spiced crab apple pickle

The miniature nature of crab apples makes them very appealing and decorative when used whole, as they are in this pickle. Different varieties of apples will give a very different look to the pickle, and small ruby red apples look particularly cute.

Keep the apples whole and leave the stalks on, then allow a few pickled apples for each serving. The apples require so little preparation that this treatment is well suited to these otherwise fiddly little fruits, but they do need to be in perfect condition before you start. You can use other apple varieties for this pickle if crab apples aren't available. Chop larger fruits, core them and pickle large chunks in the same way. Great served with cheese and biscuits.

1 Prick the apple skins with a darning needle.

2 Pour the vinegar into a stainless steel pan, add the spices and bring to the boil, then simmer for 5 minutes. Add the apples and simmer until they are tender but still hold their shape. Lift them carefully out of the vinegar using a slotted spoon and pack them into hot, sterilized jars (see page 8).

3 Add the warmed sugar to the vinegar and stir over a low heat until all the sugar has dissolved, then turn up the heat and boil steadily until the vinegar has reduced down by about a third and become syrupy.

4 Pour the hot syrup over the apples so that it completely covers them and seal the jars.

Makes 1kg (2lb 4oz)
500ml (17fl oz) cider vinegar
600g (1lb 5oz) sugar
juice and rind pared from 1 lemon, cut
    into chunks

5 whole allspice berries
2 star anise
2 dried red chillies
6 black peppercorns
1.5kg (3lb 5oz) pears

pickled pears

This is such a lovely looking pickle. The pears are wonderful eaten as a relish with cold meats and also work well with cheeses. Use up any of the sweet spiced vinegar remaining in the jar to make salad dressings. Drizzle it over a goat's cheese salad.

1 Place the vinegar, sugar, lemon rind pieces and spices in a stainless steel pan and stir over a gentle heat to dissolve the sugar. Peel and quarter the pears and toss them in the lemon juice to prevent them discolouring.

2 Place the pears in the spiced syrup and simmer gently for approximately 30 minutes until tender and translucent, depending on the ripeness of the fruit. Remove the pear pieces using a slotted spoon and place them in sterilized jars (see page 8).

3 Boil the syrup in the pan to reduce it by half, then pour it and the spices over the pears, making sure they are completely covered with the syrup. Leave until cold, then seal.

Makes about 500g (1lb 2oz)
3 plums, halved and stoned
2 apricots, halved and stoned
2 figs, halved
2 small pears, peeled and quartered

400g (14oz) sugar
juice of 1 lemon
150ml (5fl oz) dry white wine
420g (15oz) honey
50g (2oz) English mustard powder

mostarda di frutta

If you are unfamiliar with mustard fruits, now is a good time to be introduced. It is a delicious mustard-based condiment with Italian origins. (The name actually comes not from 'mustard' but from 'mosto', which is the unfermented grape juice, reduced to a thick syrup, in which the fruits were originally preserved.) Originally made with quinces or grapes, it can be made using any mixture of fruits, usually pears, plums, peaches, whole cherries and figs.

This pickle can be served chopped over fish and goes well with pork and sausages and strong salty cheeses. Finely chopped mostarda can also be mashed with pumpkin when making a filling for ravioli. Use any leftover syrup in salad dressings and drizzle over bitter salad leaves.

1 Preheat the oven to 120°C/250°F/Gas Mark ½. Place all the fruit in a stainless steel pan and add just enough water to cover.

2 Add the sugar and lemon juice and stir gently to dissolve the sugar, then turn up the heat and boil to make a thin syrup. Simmer over a low heat for about 10 minutes, so the fruit pieces are cooked but stay intact.

3 Remove the fruit pieces with a slotted spoon, draining them well, and place on a baking sheet. Cook in the oven for about 45–50 minutes until the fruits are dry.

4 Add the wine and honey to the syrup and simmer over a low heat for 10–15 minutes to reduce it down. Add the mustard powder and mix well.

5 Put the fruit pieces into hot, sterilized jars (see page 8) and pour over the syrup to cover. Leave until cold, then seal.

Makes 500g (1lb 2oz)
450g (1lb) damsons
225g (8oz) sugar
2 short cinnamon sticks

6 cloves
4 pieces of root ginger, approximately
   2cm (¾in) square
malt vinegar (for quantity see step 1)

pickled damsons

This traditional method for pickling damsons is well worth the effort. You could cut down the amount of straining and boiling, and you would still get a delicious pickle – if not quite as rich.

1 Preheat the oven to 150°C/300°F/Gas Mark 2. Put the damson into a ceramic dish and sprinkle with sugar. Tie the spices in a piece of muslin. Pour enough vinegar onto the fruit to cover it, add the bag of spices, then put the dish at the bottom of the oven for 20 minutes until the fruits feel soft and the juices start to run.

2 Allow to cool, then strain the juice into a pan and add the spices. Bring to the boil, then discard the spices and pour the liquid over the damsons. Repeat this straining and boiling process (without spices) each day for 10 days, then leave the damsons immersed in the juice for another 7 days, refrigerating between processing.

3 Strain the damsons again and pack into a hot, sterilized jar (see page 8). Bring the rich, syrupy juice to the boil and pour over the damsons. Leave until cold, then seal the jar.

Makes 500g (1lb 2oz)
450g (1lb) apricots
225g (8oz) sugar
2 short cinnamon sticks
2 cloves

2 pieces of root ginger, about
   2cm (¾in) square
½ tsp whole allspice
wine vinegar (for quantity see
   step 1 above)

pickled apricots

This is another versatile alternative, where the sweetness of the fruit is perfectly offset by the sharpness of the vinegar. Out of season, make using dried apricots instead.

Follow step 1 above, using the apricots and different spice quantities. Remove the apricots with a slotted spoon and pack into a sterilized jar (see page 8). Boil the remaining liquid until it becomes syrupy; discard the spice bag, then pour the liquid over the apricots. Leave in the fridge overnight. Next day, remove the apricots from the jar and strain the syrup into a pan. Put the apricots back in the jar and bring the syrup to the boil, then pour over the apricots. Leave until cold, then seal.

Makes 750g (1lb 10oz)
8 or 9 small lemons
sea salt (for quantity see step 2)
1 bay leaf

1 small cinnamon stick
a few coriander seeds
1 dried chilli

preserved lemons

Preserved lemons are an essential ingredient in Moroccan and North African cuisine. They can be added to casseroles and salads and have a fragrant, sweet and sour taste. Once pickled you eat the whole fruit, rind and all. As the lemons are used, simply add more salt and lemon juice to the jar so the fruits stay immersed.

1 Cut off the stalk end of each lemon; then, holding it upright, slice it down in quarters to within 2cm (¾in) of the base so it opens out but doesn't come apart.

2 Pack the sea salt in between the cuts, using approximately 1 tablespoonful for each lemon, then pack the lemons as tightly as you can into a large (approximately 1 litre/1¾ pints) sterilized wide-necked jar, pushing them down to encourage them to release their juice. Distribute the other flavourings (left whole) among the lemons. Close the jar and leave it overnight.

3 The next day, press the lemons down more so they release more juice. Continue doing this each day for the next 3 days until the lemons are completely submerged in the juice, topping up if necessary with more lemon juice.

4 Seal the jar and leave the lemons for 1 month, by which time they should be soft and ready to use.

5 Store the lemons in the refrigerator, where they will keep for at least 6 months. Rinse off excess salt before using.

Makes 2.25kg (5lb)

500g (1lb 2oz) cauliflower, broken into florets
225g (8oz) runner beans, topped
    and tailed, then sliced
225g (8oz) green tomatoes, cut into chunks
500g (1lb 2oz) shallots, peeled and halved
    if small
1kg (2lb 4oz) marrow flesh, diced
400g (14oz) salt
1.7 litres (3 pints) malt vinegar
200g (7oz) sugar
20g (¾oz) English mustard powder
10g (¼oz) mustard seeds
1 tsp ground ginger
4 small dried chillies, crushed
40g (1½oz) cornflour
15g (½oz) turmeric

piccalilli

Piccalilli is a good way of preserving homegrown seasonal vegetables, and the medley can be changed to suit what you have available at the time. It is another resourceful way of using up marrow, or you can substitute courgettes – both crops that often fit into the 'famine or feast' category: when available, there is usually an overabundance.

1 Mix all the vegetables together and layer them in a bowl, sprinkling salt in between the layers, then leave overnight. The next day, drain the vegetables, rinse thoroughly to remove all the salt and drain again.

2 Pour the vinegar into a pan and stir in the sugar, mustard powder and seeds, ginger and dried chillies. Add the vegetables and simmer until just tender but still in chunks. You can choose the texture of pickle you like best by keeping the vegetables crunchy or soft.

3 Blend the cornflour and turmeric with a few tablespoons of vinegar from the pan and stir this into the mixture, then boil for 2–3 minutes.

4 Pour the piccalilli into hot, sterilized jars (see page 8) and leave until cold, then seal.

Makes 1kg (2lb 4oz)
1kg (2lb 4oz) pickling shallots
250g (9oz) salt

600ml (1 pint) pickling vinegar
(see page 13)

pickled shallots

Pickled onions are a classic pickle and one that seems to be popular with children and adults alike. They go with just about anything, but a simple ploughman's lunch made up of a piece of crusty bread, a wedge of strong cheese and some pickled onions is a combination that is hard to beat. To be sure that your onions retain that initial crunch, they need to be marinated in brine for a few days before being packed into jars and covered in spiced vinegar. Apart from that, this pickle has to be the easiest there is and you should always keep a few jars on the pantry shelf.

1 Place the shallots in a large bowl without skinning them. Make the brine by dissolving half of the salt in 1.1 litres (2 pints) water, then pour this over the shallots and leave for 12 hours. Drain and skin the shallots.

2 Make up a second batch of brine using the remaining salt and the same amount of water, pour it over the shallots and leave for a further 2–3 days.

3 Meanwhile, if you don't already have some pickling vinegar steeping in a cupboard, make a batch of the quick version a while before the brining period is due to finish and leave until cold.

4 Drain and rinse the salt from the onions and pack them tightly into jars. Pour the cold pickling vinegar over them so that they are completely covered. Cover and seal the jars. The shallots will keep their flavour and crispness for up to 6 months after bottling.

sweet & sour onions

This pickle benefits from using a sweeter vinegar than the previous recipe, to give a delectable sweet and sour tang. It is very easy to make.

Here the onions are pickled in a sweet pickling vinegar. Follow the recipe above, but use either some sweet pickling vinegar already steeping in a cupboard or make up a batch of the quicker alternative instead (see page 13 for both recipes).

useful addresses

Many local hardware stores and well-stocked cook shops sell all the bits and pieces you need for jam making, from preserving pans to jam jars and labels. Here are a few online companies that also stock the things you will need.

www.lakeland.co.uk
www.waresofknutsford.co.uk
www.justpreserving.co.uk

JAM MAKING RESOURCE
www.jamheaven.co.uk

author's acknowledgements

Thanks to Sue Rowlands for bringing order to the proceedings, not to mention lovely props, a fabulous eye for detail and general encouragement and friendship.

Thanks also to Cindy Richards for giving me the opportunity to write a book on a subject I love, as well the rest of the Cico team; Sally Powell and Gillian Haslam for patiently pulling it all together, Alison Bolus and Eleanor Van Zandt for making sense of it all, and Jane Smith for her lovely drawings.

Thanks to Deborah Schneebeli-Morrell for making whitecurrant and chilli jam using her own homegrown fruit, and to friends and neighbours for their help and support, especially Judy Dann for our foodie conversations and for sending me surprise recipes in the post on many occasions.

Thanks to the customers of my company, The Laundry (www.thelaundry.co.uk), for being understanding when I was distracted by thoughts of jam!

Finally, a massive thank you to Chris and Lisa for helping me keep life on an even keel so I could get on with the book, and to my friend, Lindsey Stock, without whose help the book would not have been possible.

index